FROM HIDE AND HORN

A Sesquicentennial Anthology of Texas Poets

Compiled by
Peggy Zuleika Lynch
and
Edmund C. Lynch

EAKIN PRESS
Austin, Texas
1985

Library of Congress Catalogue Card Number: 85-80617

FIRST EDITION

Manufactured in the United States of America
By Eakin Publications, Inc., P.O. Box 23066, Austin, Texas 78735

ISBN 0-89015-497-X

FROM HIDE AND HORN

A Sesquicentennial Anthology of Texas Poets

Compiled by
Peggy Zuleika Lynch
and
Edmund C. Lynch

EAKIN PRESS
Austin, Texas
1985

Library of Congress Catalogue Card Number: 85-80617

FIRST EDITION

Manufactured in the United States of America
By Eakin Publications, Inc., P.O. Box 23066, Austin, Texas 78735

ISBN 0-89015-497-X

Dedicated to

Edmund's brother, Raymond Lynch, Senior
Peggy's sister, Virginia Noel
for their inspiration

CATTLE

Other states were carved or born,
Texas grew from hide and horn.

Other states are long or wide,
Texas is a shaggy hide.

Dripping blood and crumpled hair;
Some fat giant flung it there,

Laid the head where valleys drain,
Stretched its rump along the plain.

Other soil is full of stones,
Texans plow up cattle bones.

Herds are buried on the trail,
Underneath the powdered shale;

Herds that stiffened like the snow,
Where the icy northers go.

Other states have built their halls,
Humming tunes along the walls.

Texans watched the mortar stirred,
While they kept the lowing herd.

Stamped on Texan wall and roof,
Gleams the sharp and crescent hoof.

High above the hum and stir,
Jingle bridle-rein and spur.

Other states were made or born,
Texas grew from hide and horn.

Berta Hart Nance
Flute In The Distance

Contents

Preface

The idea for this anthology grew out of a casual conversation; could 150 poets be induced to write a poem on a topic related to each of the years 1836 to 1986? To find out, we sought advice from a number of established poets known to us and concluded that the idea was feasible.

In selecting poets to participate, certain considerations were established: wide geographical dispersion, as well as a wide variety of poetic styles, traditional to modern. Styles were categorized as those to be found in academe, local groups under various names, the state poetry society, and those fiercely independent. To assure that invitations went to the better poets, the primary criterion was *publication* in books, anthologies, poetry journals, or lists of winners in various national contests. Seeking the best poets, we evaluated their production as to frequency and quality by our reading and by the reviews and critiques of other poets. The respect for a prospect among local poets, as well as their activity in the support of poetry as an art form were also considerations. Participation was by invitation and less than five percent of those invited declined.

Peggy assumed responsibility for collecting the poetry, a time-consuming task which took one year of her spare time. Her extensive library of poetry books permitted much of her search to be done at home in preparing lists of potential contributors. The total list of 150 was developed piecemeal. Sometimes the invitation was extended in person at some literary conference in Texas. Often the invitation was extended after a discussion of the project by telephone. The formal invitation was then issued. There were hours devoted to persuading the fainthearted or urging on the laggards. She lived with this anthology for over a year. Her primary interest was in the poets and their poetry.

Edmund was responsible for the general plan of the anthology and the writing of the prose sections. His work included the design of the letter of invitation and the helpful hints to guide the poet in search of a topic. He used his spare time for several months reading Texas history to prepare for writing the concise summaries that precede each chapter as a background for the specific eras. His primary interest was to assist the reader through visual appeal and clarity of presentation.

We foresaw from the beginning that the poetic mind, given free reign, would result in a unique view of Texas history as they applied their imagination and sensibility to their chosen topics. The reader is invited to enjoy the fruits of their effort and to explore the development of Texas over 150 years as portrayed by poetic minds.

THE BRIDE THAT I WOO IS DANGER

Give to the poet his well earned praise,
 And the songs of his love, preserve them;
Encircle his brows with fadeless bays,
 The children of genius deserve them;
But never to me such praises breathe,
 To the minstrel-feeling a stranger —
I only sigh for the laurel-wreath
 That a patriot wins in DANGER.

Speed, speed the day when to war I hie!
 The fame of the field is inviting.
Before my sword shall foemen fly,
 Or fall in the flash of its lightning.
Away with song and away with charms!
 Insulted Freedom's proud avenger,
I bear no love but the love of arms,
 And the bride that I woo is DANGER.

When shall I meet the audacious foe,
 Face to face where the flags are flying?
I long to thin them, "two at a blow,"
 And ride o'er the dead and the dying!
My sorrel steed shall his fetlocks stain
 In the brain of the hostile stranger;
With an iron heel he spurs the plain,
 And he breathes full and free in DANGER.

When victory brings the warrior rest,
 Rich the rewards of martial duty —
The thanks of a land with freedom blest,
 And the smiles of its high-born beauty.
Does victory fail? — enough for me
 That I fall not to fame a stranger;
His name shall roll with eternity
 Who finds the foremost grave in DANGER.

Mirabeau B. Lamar
Second President,
Republic of Texas

Introduction

This poetic anthology is a tribute to the Sesquicentennial of Texas by poets of Texas. Each poet was invited to select and to write a poem related to a significant event or person for one of the years 1836 to 1986. A poetic view of Texas history is presented in the contemporary vernacular. Since "Texas grew from hide and horn," it was no easy task to round up one hundred and fifty Texas poets — dogies, mavericks and trail-worn longhorns — to make contributions to this sesquicentennial volume. And since Texans are known for their frontier, independent spirit, the reference to the pioneer cattle industry and to Berta Hart Nance's classic poem, is as comfortable and fitting as a pair of custom-made cowboy boots.

What was the status of poetry in the early days of the Republic? The Texians who migrated from areas east of the Mississippi River seeking adventure and a better life brought with them the traditions of their origins, primarily from the Old South. Philip Graham identifies the southern cavalier and southern puritan cultures among them. The southern cavalier culture could be identified by the spirit of war which was glorified by an ideal of liberty and sanctified by defense of home. Emphasis on religion enabled the pioneers to cope with their daily hardships and loneliness through its consolation and moralizing. Early Texas verse was conventional in spirit and imitative in form and manner. As might be expected, patriotic verse was numerous and followed the cavalier tradition. There was a dearth of love poems in the early days.

The Texians had little time or inclination for poetry. Households were widely dispersed, villages were small, schools and libraries lacking. The literary spark was kept alive by the editors of the newspapers that emerged to disseminate news and to inform this scattered population. Such papers had their "Poet's Corner" with one or more poems, often anonymous, in each issue.

It is interesting to note that the second President of the Republic of Texas, Mirabeau B. Lamar, wrote *The Bride That I Woo Is Danger** during his first visit to Texas in 1835. Lamar was then an established poet and this poem is an example of the cavalier tradition, speaking of deeds of chivalry, combat and its dangers. This poem was published in the *Texas Republican* at Brazoria, October 10, 1835.

The poems in this anthology are presented in sections, each marking a significant era in the development of Texas. A concise narrative summary precedes each section to provide a backdrop for the poetry. The summaries speak primarily of the people, their culture and their livelihood.

*Philip Graham, *Early Texas Verse (1835–1850)*, The Steck Company, 1936.

I
Republic and Statehood 1836–1859

Texians migrated from Alabama, Georgia, Mississippi and Tennessee seeking adventure and a better life — bringing with them their culture of the Old South based on agriculture and slavery. They were highly individualistic with a strong distaste for governmental intervention in their lives. This desire for independence and disinterest in government was not understood by the Mexican officials. Such attitudes marked Texians as a breed apart.

The government of the Republic of Texas was no more than needed and was marked by grand ideas with little money to carry them out. Conflicts with Mexico and the Indians were a continuing problem, complicated by the status of Indians beyond the Texas border as wards of the Federal Government.

Statehood brought a steady increase in population from other states and from Middle Europe. The early settlements were east of the ninety-eighth meridian, roughly a line from San Antonio to Fort Worth.

Subsistence farming was the rule with each community self-sufficient. Pioneer women worked side by side with the men. As the population grew, cotton and corn were cultivated for export to add to cattle products such as hides, tallow and salt beef. It was an era of general prosperity for the individual based on agriculture.

THE FOLKS WHO CAME TO TEXAS

The wagons rolled from out the South;
they came from Tennessee
to find new land and make a home
and live where men were free.

The wagons came from way back East,
Kentucky, Alabam'.
They came to great, wide open space
to build their brand new towns.

Sam Houston came in 'thirty-two
and got himself some fame
For beating Santa Anna's men;
they gave a town his name.

The Lone Star rose across the land.
A new nation was born
where buffalo and Indians lived
among mesquite and thorns.

The early settlers learned to live
with people they found here.
Tejanas, Spanish, Mexicans
helped out the pioneers.

So those brave men and women, too,
conquered the wild frontier
to raise their steers and make their homes
through many long, lean years.

The folks began to look ahead;
the time for union came.
In 'forty-five they joined the states,
but kept their Texas name.

Then others came from North and East:
Dutchmen, Germans, Irish, too,
Africans, Danes and Englishmen,
Italians, Czechs and Jews.

All together they built the state
and pledged their loyalty
to the big land of Redbird's song
and Bluebonnets in spring.

Dorothy Lee Hansen

THE REPUBLIC

There was a mighty upheaval down Texas way
Where bluebonnets bloomed and fast guns held sway
The battles were over and independence had come
The flag of the Republic waved its star in the sky
Signalling to all the Republic's birth.

Then the doors were opened near and far
For finding the way to the Great Lone Star.
They were to come by the thousands
A mixture of settlers, families, and loners,
To the caprock mountains and the Indian trails
To the cattle barons' prairies
Where the wild wolf wails,
Facing the desert's challenge
And the sandstorm gales.

Free and independent with village centered culture
They quickly would learn by laws to abide
For the Texas lawmen would ride far and wide.

Longing to be tied to the land of the free
The courageous settlers wanted to be
A part of the Union that bound men together.
Those who were yankees and had been born to such kin
Soon blessed the Union that Texas went in.

Houston, Austin, Lamar, illustrious statesmen all,
Making history.
1836, the year of new birth!

Catherine Case Lubbe

1837

THE TEXAS NAVY

The *Brutus* and *Invincible* were sleek, swift men-of-war,
Patrolling schooners, off the Texas coast.
They paralyzed old Mexico's proud merchant marine fleet
And captured bounty of which they would boast.
But of the Texas Navy, only these two now,
With angry waters breaking on each bow.

In August of that fateful year the *Brutus* brought a prize
To Galveston, across the treacherous Bar . . .
The Mexican *Abispa*, seized by a jubilant crew
And Captain James D. Broyland, for the Star.
Yes, of the Texas Navy there are but two ships now
With angry waters breaking on each bow.

Across the bar at sea the ship *Invincible* remained
Awaiting better tides to cross next day,
But brigs *Iturbide* and *Liberatadore* launched attack
And on the bar another victim lay.
So of the Texas Navy there is just one ship now
With angry waters breaking on the bow.

In coming to the rescue, the *Brutus*, too, was caught
Upon the bar, but somehow got away
To meet her ruin later in a storm — an "act of God" —
At anchor in October in the bay.
And so these Texas naval stars and stripes fly nevermore
And angry waves break only on the shore.

Jean Calkins

INAUGURATION TEXAS STYLE

Too much "higgling," the Republic of Texas said.
So on victor Lamar's inauguration day
came Samuel Houston, its erstwhile president,
costumed in jest as old George Washington.
The sight of Old Grizzly brought back the fiery times
and men who ousted him now rose and cheered.
"Remember the Alamo!" (and San Jacinto, too.)
"Speech! Speech!" they begged Old Sam. He spoke,
recalling all the men he knew and loved,
the hard and good times shared, the pain, the glory.

This was a president's farewell speech, he said.
Did he explain his "higgling" was purely patience,
same patience that won at San Jacinto bend
and kept exploiters from bilking the young Republic?
Did he boast that though the cost was blood
the many journals sprung up this very year
were theirs to use as voices of liberty?

Mirabeau Buonaparte Lamar, new-made chief,
could finally rise to speak his eloquent words.
With men's unselfish aid he would promote
the talent, wealth and enterprise of Texas,
not as part of those United States
whose Congress under John Q. Adams's goad
had spurned their selfless annexation bid
(which Anson Jones, their man in Washington,
had now withdrawn, "final and absolute.")
The young Republic of Texas could stand alone
to send a flood of light throughout the world . . .

President Lamar, philosopher, patriot, poet,
father of Texas schools and Texas pride,
a civilized and civilizing man,
finished and bowed, and bowing brought to life
the first new deal in Texas.

Gladys Gassman

1839

SOMEONE MUST DREAM THE DREAM

Mirabeau Buonaparte Lamar in 1839

See them down there around the beast
I have just slain! They seem astounded
that the Poet–President of the Republic
could fell the largest bison bull ever seen
by a Texian! They may not comprehend my verses
but they fathom my success on the hunt. I smile;
this lucky deed may give me more leverage with them.
They motion me to come — I should be rushing down
to place my boot on my prize — do they think me
hesitant to see the shaggy mammoth heave
his last blood? Yes, I would rather be
at my books, but this is a rough world.
I will be down in a moment.

But for the moment, let me linger on this hill
where that serene valley stretches before me.
I dream of lands beyond the far mountains
that could be ours, an empire from the Gulf
to the Pacific! And this place where I stand,
it is noble enough for the building
of a capitol here. Our capitol!
I can hear the trumpets already!
We shall call our city for Austin.

Yes, yes, I am coming. But I have visions
of glory for my people . . . someone must dream
the dream. Now that our homesteads are secure
by law, libraries and schools shall rise.
Our children must be able to hold the pen
if they hold the reins of this empire.
And perhaps . . . perhaps some child
out of this generation or the next
will write verses to glorify
all that we are.

Yes, yes, I am starting down to make
the first cut! But up here on my hill
I have looked out to the wide, rolling future!

Violette Newton

THE DISPOSSESSED

[*The Indians are tenants at will, and have no possessory rights.*
— Mirabeau Buonaparte Lamar,

Injured peace finds ways to bleed,
And dispossessed know well the need for war.
So when in San Antonio that day in March the two sides met,
They knew the threads were thin that held the hope of peace.
Sixty-five Comanche met, Maguara at the head,
With scores of whites, there to talk of peace, but ready for a fight.
Then came Maguara's lie, *We have one captive, only one!*
Yet she was there, the child Matilda Lockhart — two years' captive
In the redskin camp — to shriek the truth, *There are others!*
The Council House that should have been a place of pride
Became instead a place of bloody death for twenty whites
And twice as many of the dispossessed.

A vengeful, deadly summer raid was all the hope Comanches had —
They killed and plundered, stole and burned across the valley
Of the Guadalupe, through Linville and Victoria on the coast.
They must have known that Texas had not room enough
For all the hate, for all the spilled blood Mirabeau Lamar
Had urged. They must have known that their retreat
Could not escape the white man's armies — men under Huston,
Burleson, Colonel Moore. And soon the end was near.
Plum Creek near Lockhart — and where Colorado City stands today
Comanches fell like dying buffalo beneath the white man's guns.
Many shared the blame of blood that year — McCloud, McCulloch,
William Cooke, the Texas Rangers, Travis Guards. Lamar, of course.

Yet while the blood soaked darkly into Texas's war-raged dust,
Happier flowers bloomed across the Texas soil:
The land became more safe for immigrants, surveyors
Flooding now in record numbers, bringing with them hope
For more than death — hope for culture in the wild West.
In Austin, the new capital, the Austin Lyceum was formed
To cultivate young, eager minds, and teach, perhaps,
That music, art, and books speak just as loud as guns.
Across East Texas, newspapers sprung like oases to quench
The basic need of all mankind for truth;
And in that truth, the injured peace found ways to mend,
To form the tapestry that someday would become a state.

Gene Fehler

THE BEGINNINGS OF HIGHER EDUCATION IN TEXAS

From Tennessee to Texas for ninety days they traveled with a sick baby.
Down the broad Mississippi they came to be missionaries to
the Indians in the Indian Territory.
They were John Witherspoon Pettigrew McKenzie and his wife Matilda.
The baby Martha Elizabeth survived although there had been doubts
and fears.

By the mercy of God the paddlewheeler they rode reached
a landing where the Red River joined the Mississippi. They
disembarked and got to the small village of Clarksville
although this entailed overland travel by wagon.

Circuit riding was J.W.P.'s duty for a few years.

But this highly educated man yearned to be a teacher.
He knew the frontiersmen and women needed and wanted their
children to have an education.

English, Latin, Greek, algebra, calculus haunted his dreams.

He took 16 boys into his home for a start. Then as his reputation
grew so did his school, to a peak enrollment of 400.

Boys from Texas, Louisiana, Mississippi, even from Missouri,
came to him for learning. Boys who walked or rode horses for
a hundred miles or more.

Boys who worked at cutting trees for tuition, buildings,
books and food. Boys who were willing to endure any
inconvenience in order to sit in a class under him.

For twenty-five years McKenzie College educated boys:
future ministers, bishops of the church, publishers, teachers,
lawyers, and businessmen of Texas and surrounding states.

A final farewell to the college J.W.P. McKenzie loved and
nursed into being was given this institution in 1869.
One of the finest institutions in the South was destroyed
by the Civil War.

Never mind the hostile Indians, the floods, the famines,
the outlaw gangs that roamed the Red River territory.
Civil War and Reconstruction Days did it in.

Beth Bryant Brady

SEPTEMBER SCENE

[*In September 1842, fifty-three Texas soldiers, led by Nicholas Dawson, were attacked by Mexican troops near the Salado River. Overpowered, the Texans surrendered, only to have thirty-five men butchered in what was dubbed the Dawson Massacre.*]

September is a golden time
when leaves
drift red
in gentle reunion
with earth . . .
of long oak shadows —
balm
for fading grass.

Somewhere.

Not here.

This weeded field
is softened
only by clustered mesquite
which wrestles with sod
for the right to live.
Branches clash
in a cloudless sky
(scant shelter for a soldier
under fire).
Here thirty-five men,
like leaves
yielding to September,
fell red . . .
in reunion
with earth.

Ghosts
scream in sequence
like bullets
from a rifle.

Mary Canizaro

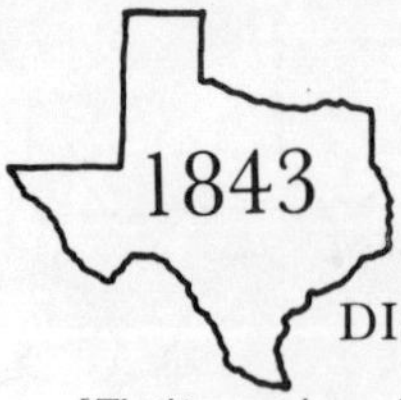

DISPLACEMENTS — 1843 or thereabouts

[*The things you have said are not sweet like sugar but bitter like gourds. You said that you wanted to put us upon a reservation, to build us houses and make us medicine lodges. I do not want them. I was born upon the prairie where the wind blew free and there was nothing to break the light of the sun.*

— Ten Bears of the Root Eaters]

About then they were heading this way,
my ancestors trying to homestead a section
or two in Bosque County. In County Clare
such acres would have meant wealth,
station. Not so here for these luckless farmers.

My dead kin tried and failed: potatoes easy
and too cheap, cotton responsive to weevils,
peanuts yet distant prophecy for this sandy loam.
Assessing my dead kin I try to image
our mutual land, a century and more separating,

uniting. I wonder if they affirmed Lamar's epigram:
The cultivated mind is the guardian genius of democracy.
I doubt it. My father, poor white out of Bosque County
lucky for his sixth-grade schooling, told me
to get an education and never be beholden
to any bastard. My father's motives
weren't mainly I think the cultivated mind.

Sixth-grader long ago I puzzle past,
inchoate present. I'd like to think some one
of my ancestors greedy for his section reckoned
the meaning of claims. Later, Comanches
would have an eloquent spokesman whom I've read:

my father didn't nor would he have spoken
poetically of these worlds colliding — my ancestors,
my father, these Indians all displaced, displacing
and leaving curious heirs. Among my annual gifts
is a check to Indian charities. Never enough

even as token: my people presaging those
who would claim in fee simple these prodigal acres
Indians claimed rightfully unclaimed
because nothing should break the light of the sun.

Arguments can go either way. I wonder how my father,
my ancestors, those Irish arguers buried near the Bosque,
measured losers, victors, themselves: nothing left now
except this mortgaged understanding.

Betsy Colquitt

THE LAST PRESIDENT

Imagine that 1844 Inaugural Day,
Washington-on-the-Brazos, Texas capitol,
fog seeps in and out riverbanks. In blue norther cold,
women stuff rags in chinks between cabin walls.
A crowd huddles outside Major Hatfield's log saloon.
Legislators and wives, cotton farmers, new settlers, slaves
wait shivering, expectant of what might come.
Up outer stairs, the outgoing President climbs.
Sam Houston, raucous voice soft in defeat,
gives his farewell address, "If we remain a nation
our territory will reach to the Pacific shores."
"You tell 'em Sam," a frontiersman yells.

Honorable Anson Jones, new President,
red hair flaming, against a sky lead-gray,
orates at the podium. Possessed of a schoolmaster's face,
this physician, transplanted from New England soil,
speaks nothing of annexation to the states.
"O, Providence," he prays. "Protect our Texas land."

Ladies in crinoline, gentlemen in cravats,
dance to a fiddler's tune at the Inaugural Ball
in Hatfield's second floor Representatives' Hall.
Young James K. Holland laughs at one incident.
As fiddlers tune up, a girl in full petticoats
starts out with him to join in a lively gavotte.
She extends no arm, sinking instead down through the floor
midway to the saloon below. General Chambers helps
pull her up. Carpenters neglected to nail down boards.
President Jones stands with dignity, stiffly reserved,
greets all revelers. Weight of office hangs
heavy like clouds of stone over his head.

This night of cruel weather, chilled to his marrowbones,
he rides a horse back to his plantation house.
Mary, his wife, is expecting their third-born child.
Between trees, black with boughs, one star winks out.

In some reflective trance he hears the wind sing,
"Shine Union of Stars, Star of Texas, shine"

Dorothy E. Combs

TEXAS JOINS THE UNION

Once claimed by France and then by Spain,
And Mexico's Federation,
The new Republic of Texas
Pondered U.S. annexation.

This was in Eighteen Forty-five,
And on July 4th (historic date),
Texans resolved in Convention
To join the Union as a State.

Delegates labored on the terms:
Her public lands would be retained,
And from the area, by consent,
At least four States could be obtained.

On the 13th of October,
Its Constitution was ratified;
As it met U.S. requirements,
President Polk was satisfied.

He signed the Annexation Bill
Before December ended,
And the bright Lone Star of Texas
To Old Glory was appended.

Mildred Vorpahl Baass

STAGECOACH ROAD

Sleeping now in shadows
this stretch of ancient road,
etched long ago by pounding hooves and turning wheels
deep into the sandy hills of East Texas,
still dreams of Pioneers.

Here, watched by unseen Indians,
the apprehensive settlers chopped a trail
from Marshall's thriving village
to the steamboat landing at Port Caddo.

Down this forgotten trace moved
the meager commerce of early Texas.
Men with muskets came this way
to join the struggling Texians in their cause.
Here Bradfield's creaking stage
lumbered west from Shreveport,
to meet the Butterfield Express at Marshall,
carrying drifters and dreamers and builders
into the newborn state.

But now they come no more.
Gone are the drifters and the dreamers,
Gone the settlers who stopped a while
to build their cabins here.
Gone are the woodsmen and the plowmen and
the mothers singing to their frightened children
in the night.

Today along this ghostly road
nothing remains but little mounds
of fallen chimney stones and unmarked graves.
Yet in the lonely silence you can almost hear
the Caddo's muffled footfalls
and the westbound stagecoach passing
round the bend.

James M. Thomas

1847

THE "IN" PLACE

Significant in Texas memorabilia of 1847 was the emergence of Nimitz Steamboat Hotel in Fredericksburg as a landmark — as the "in" place for smart travelers . . . And for nearly a century and a half the Nimitz — with its unique front built to resemble a ship's prow — has appeared ready to set sail down the Hill Country town's Main Street . . .

The structure was designed by Charles Nimitz, a German soldier turned colonizer, to perpetuate his love of the sea. Among its famed guests were General Robert E. Lee and President Rutherford B. Hayes . . .

Still dominating the downtown scene, the hotel is now a museum in Nimitz Center. The Center was established as a memorial to the elder Nimitz's grandson, Admiral Chester Nimitz, Commander of the Pacific Fleet in WW II . . .

It is one of many historic inns of the state. Some have been restored, some are museums, and others are restaurants. But all are reminders of a way of life which no longer exists such as: . . . Hotel Texas, Fort Worth, *Home of the Cattle Barons*; Excelsior House, Jefferson, *Gateway to Texas*; The Adolphus, Dallas, *Beautiful Lady with a Past*; Hotel Galvez, Galveston, *Queen of the Gulf* . . .

Tarpon Inn, Port Aransas, where FDR loved to fish; The Driskill, Austin, almost a *Second Statehouse*; Rice Hotel, Houston (The Rice *WAS* Houston); Nutt House, Granbury — hotwater corn bread
and opera . . .

Landmark Inn, Castroville, *An Inn Locked in Time,* Hotel Genocchio, Marshall, *Ghosts, Graves and Tunnels*; . . . and many others, each adding its own bit of Texana luster.

Ruth Grundy

THE ROAD

The war with Mexico is done with,
everything in this great harsh country ours,
sun-drenched, poisonous, blossoming, mud-scarred,
north of the Rio Grande.
This is the year of trails that don't quite work
from waterhole to waterhole
to wide simmering deserts that kill the animals.
A long year
laying the foundation for trails that work
across West Texas to the fort at Franklin,
all the way to California.
That road is still a dream, littered with corpses
we can't believe are ours.
Roads blazed through difficult passes
end in three walls of solid rock.

Some of us make it through
by the grace of accident.
The springs we need
are unmarked, hidden, not on any map.
Mountains approach, discover they exist
in our lives.
Through treacherous Limpia Canyon, we follow the stream
to camp in Wild Rose Pass. Clouds, pure white,
solid, substantial,
balance above the mountains
as if stone talked to stone
with centuries to wait for answers,
to endure if no answer comes
beyond this wholeness.
Stone, cloud.

We call the stars.
They come close as breathing.
It's a dream, like the wild belief
the body will last, our blood racing under these blankets
under the Milky Way,
stars long gone like eyes from their sockets.
We dream of going further
than we ever have. For water
we drink the juice of prickly pear.
News comes through of gold
found at Sutter's Mill.
But not for gold would we give our lives.
More than we dream of gold or stars
we dream of this road
that is worth what we give it.

Del Marie Rogers

TEXAS 1849

Gold. Suddenly, all trails
led to California streams
flowing with gold

like honey. Even the new path
to El Paso took them away,
men who never meant to settle.

This year the State claimed
Texas along the Rio Grande,
El Paso north to Santa Fe.

But even the Governor's "whole
power" could not persuade
the President or Santa Fe.

West Texas was the Llano Estacado,
not Cibola.
Meanwhile, near Nacogdoches,

B. F. and Sarah Jackson
laid their youngest son to rest
under the cool pine clay,

all gold in California
nothing to them, Santa Fe
only another foreign post.

Here they meant to raise their only
children growing faster than pines.
On the grave of David

they swore their faith in all
things here, they squeezed
each other's hands and stayed.

Walter McDonald

PADRE ISLAND
(Then and Now)

A bar of gold along the Texas coast.
Island of intrigue, wealth and mystery.
Your reckless past a legendary ghost
That harbors secrets of your history.

For centuries you were a pawn of chance,
Exploited by whomever chanced to find
Himself a guest of yours by circumstance.
You hosted every breed of humankind.

The years before you wore the Texas Brand
Were lawless. Even when Texas came to view
You as her own you flaunted contraband
Of greed, conspiracy and rendezvous.

Wealth-laden ships were dashed against your shore
Spilling rare treasures from exotic lands
To form a carpet on your ocean floor.
Men buried gold deep in your lonely sands.

Echoes of dissonance have died away.
No longer are there conquests to be won.
Yet something clings, some restless disarray,
Some wheel of fortune waiting to be spun.

Sophisticated now, prim and demure,
Smug in your sun-resort complacency.
Deep down inside still pregnant with the lure
Of buried gold. And so it well may be
That someday men will tap your hidden gold,
But never tap your personality.

Christine Rosamond Stedman

1851

THE DAY OF SMALL THINGS

[. . . *the day of small things*
— Zechariah 4:10]

Good years are missed by history books,
For history looks at wrecks and wars and stress and storms.
Good years are busy in unnoticed nooks,
Like graveyards, bedrooms, bookshelves, shops, and roads, and farms.
The obits said that *Leatherstocking*'s Cooper died,
And Audubon drew his last bird and breath,
And whole-grain-cracker Graham, the health food man, fell,
Awkwardly, at only fifty-five. Newspapers thrive on death.
Obstetrics columns do not sell;
So Wall Street's Dow and bookman Dewey were denied
Announcements of their birth. The papers also failed to tell
The future worth of Hawthorne's latest tale
About the seven-gabled house, or Melville's great white whale.

In Galveston, Gail Borden pressed dried meat
And took the biscuit to the first world's fair
In London's Crystal Palace. It won the premium there
Beside McCormick's rig for reaping wheat,
And India rubber cloth (for blimps?), Charles Goodyear's feat.

The wagons rolled through Clarksville,
About thirty or forty a day,
West toward fertile Three Forks till
State headcounts grew thirteen percent,
In spite of AWOL slaves who went
By hundreds down toward Monterey
In Mexico, where riskful freedom lay.

A Negro felon, sent to Huntsville's pen,
Enraged the white ones there, but scored
A little first for all his race;
And cows and corn and cotton poured
From Texas lands at record pace.
So histories try to tell us when
The great things happen — but we, tritely, know
That, still, great oaks from acorns grow,
And growing roots can split a rock
Without the noise of lightning's shock.

George Wilmeth Ewing

FORT CLARK

The measured march of ghostly regiments,
The cadence of slow drums against the night,
A bugle's grievous funeral taps at dawn,
A half-staffed flag unfurled to the sky —
Defiance to a Lipan arrow's flight.

The sagas of the gala and the dance,
A single glass of wine to toast a bride,
A Seminole who lies in alien ground,
The Widow Boyd whose heart was numb with grief,
The fort, a landmark of a people's pride.

So still Las Moras flows her seaward way,
She is not heedless of the tow'ring oaks,
The rich pecans; nor of the multitude
Of speechless things — the stomping doe, the buck
Unsighted in the graying browse, the quail
Whose song has graced the day; the great bronze bird
So difficult to see, the hawk whose prey,
An hour ago was singing in the sky —
Edentate mammal of an ancient age;
Nor of the planets, Jupiter or Mars,
Orion's Belt, the polar star, the moon,
The sun which had been God to many men
Who trod her banks.

Listen, listen, ye who come here:
Greet ye the ghosts of Las Moras.
Listen, listen, ye who cross here:
Listen, listen, greet ye the stillness.
Listen.

John Halliday McCormick

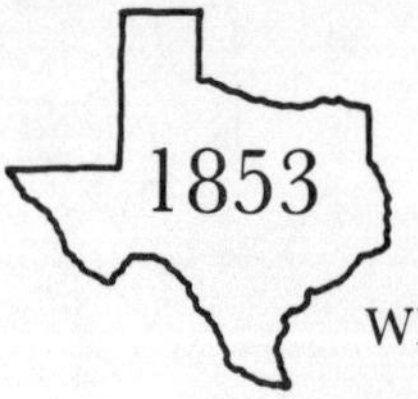

WHEELER SHANNON, TEXAS HERO

Wheeler came to Texas
to make his home, to settle
and raise kids and cows and hogs.
But first he took his place
within the Ranger band
whose fame soon would spread.

He worked with Mr. Neighbors,
Agent to the Tribes out west,
and helped elect Elisha Pease.
And never holding to party lines,
was known alike by Know-Nothings and by Whigs
as one who kept his promise.

When Congress called,
Wheeler went with Captain Pope
to survey Marcy Trail
and find a western route for rails.
He went because as scout
he had knowledge of the land,
but more, the chiefs of every band would greet
their friend and take his hand
as one who kept his promise.

Wheeler did his job well,
and as they sat at campfires at night
to tell of exploits,
he thought of kids and cows and hogs,
and knew that they must wait;
some promises could never come
until the Law was safe
and the Army stayed
and extreme things had all been done.
But on the trail one night,
the snake beneath the log
ended Wheeler's dreams
of kids and cows and hogs.

Gilbert Benton

LA REUNION

Victor Considerant seeking a place to establish a commune,
chose the hills west of the village of Dallas;
he returned to his native France to recruit immigrants;
embellished by his oratory, his land of promise became a reality
when French, Swiss, and Belgian families joined the project.
The first group arrived in April 1854, they were not farmers
or tradesmen but aristocrats, musicians, artists and jewelers
and physicians; this socialistic commune was to share and share alike,
raise their food from the land and build their houses working together.
Difficulties developed, the soil was shallow over rocks, not suited
to producing, drouths came, winters were harsh, the people suffered
hardships; they became discontented with the colony life.
In 1857 the commune was a failure and it was dissolved.
Some of the families returned to their native land, others
relocated in other parts of Texas, and New Orleans claimed some.
Some joined the inhabitants of the Dallas village of farmers,
tradesmen, cowboys and other pioneers, reverting to their
individual talents, these artisans of the dissolved commune,
became physicians, musicians, artists and forgot the Utopia
promised by Victor Considerant, the community of Dallas grew;
Revershon, a botanist, had a park named for him, the names of
Santerre, Allrye Bureau, Ben Lang, Brisbane and others were
woven into the history of Dallas, leaving footprints of their
culture in their contribution to the Dallas village.
The descendants of La Reunion colonists can be found today
but the only remaining landmark of the French colony is
the Fishtrap Cemetery, a grim reminder of the past.

Faye Carr Adams

THE CAMELS

[*Jefferson Davis, Secretary of War, authorized an experiment to determine the suitability of camels for military transport in West Texas. The Confederates dispersed the camels in 1861.*]

"I seen them once," the wizened
old settler told his wide-eyed
captive audience of early Texans.
"They wuz called 'Camels' by the ones
who rode them, them Arab fellows,
and they had long necks, and a hump
on their backs. They wuz brought
here to Texas by this feller named Davis,
who had them shipped to Indianola,
a seaport on the Gulf."

"I seen them, and I heard they wuz to go
in caravans across the Rockies
clear to Californy." The old man
told his listeners he once lived
near Camp Verde in Kerr County
in the early days of the state,
and the camels were there.

"They wuz tall, and the soldiers said
they could go for days without water.
They wuznt like anything I ever seen
before or since, and the year
wuz 1855, somewhere abouts."
"Of course, it could'a been a dream,
but it warnt. I know for sure
they wuz real, cause I wuz there,
and one of them bit me,
the ungrateful critter,
when I offered him a chaw
of my tobaccy." "On top 'o that,
I never got to ride one
of them long-legged, long-necked
freaks o' nature."

Vera L. Eckert

LOS CHISOS
(an event of 1856)

The stones cry out.
You smoke your last cigarette.
All the others wet.

And listen.
To the stones. While heat rips the river.
Water taken in sadness. Old men talk.

There were oaks at the river.
And rocks. Rocks of sixty million years.
Lichened.
They brought the girl here.
Required her to ride a hard horse through miles of mesquite.
Made her get down. Let her bathe.

Dumb phallus over the slow flow.
Horses pissing in the dirt.
Girl's father dead at the ranch. His throat gashed.

Now. Old men. Only winds.
The bandits long gone. Cheated of their girl.
One Maria. Afloat. Dead in the water. Her breasts flat.
And no sky watching.

Robert Burlingame

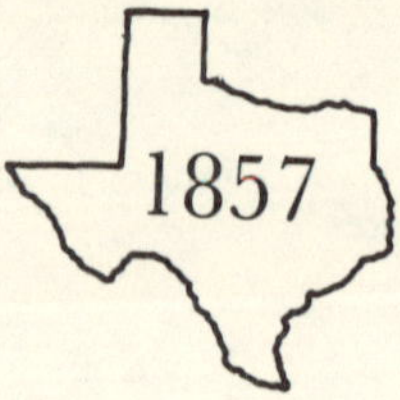

GENESIS OF TEXAS

The year was 1857. The infancy of railroads
slowly etched its way across the untamed heart of
Texas. With primitive implements tracks were
laid over hill and river, ravine and plain.

Brawny men mixed sweat and soil as they cut
through age-old timber, brush, stone — At night
they lay on hard, hard beds, too tired to be wary
of tarantulas crawling, wild animals, unfriendly
Indians, Mexicans marauding, sounds of coyotes yelping,
night birds calling, restless horses tramping, cattle
bawling . . . to awaken to pleasant aroma of hoecakes
cooking on open fires.

James Birch created a mail route — four-horse
coaches, room for mail, six passengers, six-shooters
ready for Indian attacks along the trail.

The Cart War between Texan and Mexican teamsters raged,
angry shouts, wheels and guns profaned the air along
freight trails south of San Antonio until Elisha Pease
called out the militia to stop the bloody brawl.

The Know-Nothing Party rose to political prominence;
but fell to two-times Governor Pease who secured the
Texas permanent school fund, and the granting of land
to railroads, while arguments over slavery and cessation
began to increase.

The year is 1984. The railroad pioneers struggled to
gain with all they had of brawn and brain, have been
dwindling away — a slow decay. The highways are clogged
with trucks, buses — jets thunder over our heads, the
shuttle has become matter of fact, our state schools are in
jeopardy, evolution and humanism have taken full sway.
Christian schools spring up to compensate.

The pensive sounds of train whistles seldom beckon on
the limitless Texas air. Yet, the romance of trains still
lives in the hearts of historians. The struggle to bring
prayer back into state schools is not ended. The misfire
of eleven guns cannot sink a battleship eighty percent strong,
nor, with God at the helm, can be kept at bay for long.

Kathleen Henry Harris Curry

1858

ROUND TOP: MICROCOSM OF AMERICA

On the old San Felipe trail at Cummins Creek crossing
John Myers Jones offered postal service and refreshment
From a carefully crafted round-topped dwelling,
Circular lookout providing advance notice,
Hostile or friendly, red or white or brown,
Later a decent watering hole for day riders
Halfway between Houston and Austin on the Colorado.
A blood offering of firstborn paid San Jacinto:
Robison, Winburn, and the brothers Townsend.
Younger survivors joined Santa Fe and Snively,
Returning with tall tales of deserts and canyons
Longer and wider and higher than prairie eye had seen.
A favored few fancied the ripe, rolling bottomland,
Lingering for a brief, splendid generation
To build a fragile, glittering empire
Of cotton, gentility, and education:
Round Top Academy, 1854, *mens sana in corpore sano,*
For a decade, like fated Indian summer, bright beacon
Lighting fertile prairies where whiskered gentlemen
Erected Corinthian monuments of native wood and stone,
Needing fresh whitewash after the great gray loss.
Quickly, like a hot August wind,
Plantations metamorphose into foursquare farms,
Sold part by parcel for inflated greenbacks
To stalwart Deutschlanders with guttural surnames,
Saluting neither blue nor gray, seeing
In the black pregnant soil shadows
Of a fatherland remembered, erecting
Double log cottages with mud and daub chimneys,
Prairie pioneers whose third and fourth generations
Gladly transfer allegiance to red and white and blue,
Press Aryan chins low to the solid earth,
Proudly translating hymns and names
Into patriotic, pronounceable American English.

James Darrell Skaggs

TO TEXAS IN 1859

Her given name was Henrietta Hope;
We loved her, and we dared to call her Grandma;
Revered by all, she was the family queen
Who ruled her family, including Grandpa.

A farmer's wife and hardy pioneer,
She gathered eggs and cooked and made her soap;
She birthed and raised her children, twelve in number,
And did so with a sense of humor and hope.

She came to Texas in a wagon train
When savage Indians scourged the countryside
And she was just a little girl of five —
Arriving in a country wild and wide.

She came to Texas in 1859
And stayed in Texas till 1952;
She left a heritage of work and honor
To those who loved her and called her Grandma too.

Jim Tom Barton

DARK THREATENINGS GROW

The harvesttime had passed in 1860
when John Cooper carried his son to the field
and gazed upon unplowed stubbled rows.
He spoke of things beyond the young boy's grasp,
"It will not be like this in 1861,
you and I, your mother, all of us
who plant the fertile fields and reap good crops.

"Texans are changing now that Sam Houston lost
the chance for president. Abe Lincoln holds
the power for peace, or war, and he will bind
the Union in a mighty force at any cost.
Dark threatenings grow and reason dies.

"The South believes it has the final word
over people's lives. They'd keep the Union,
yes, in lesser power. Texas wavers,
most never cared for slavery since they love
freedom more. My son, Sam Houston nursed
the infant Texas through its birth and then
to proud statehood, put down insurrections,
made the land a place to live in peace,
but he is old and people will not heed
his wise advice, his way that is the best.

"My son, you will not remember this, but you
must be the man in charge when war breaks out.
For Texas surely will secede and fight
against a stronger North, cool, determined
to win the war and they have other reasons,
debts they'll never pay if they can win.

"Someday there shall be peace on earth again,
goodwill for neighbors. Like our Governor Sam,
I seek Divine guidance and you must, too.
Remember, a man who owns a slave becomes
a slave himself for none is free unless
all are free. When Texas calls I must
respond and serve. These fields, though sown in lead
and wetted down in blood, strewn with bones
will wait for seed to grow that you can plant,
when peace returns and healing has its way."

Roberta Pipes Bowman

II
Confederacy and Reconstruction 1860–1875

Texas seceded and joined the Confederacy because the Old South influence was dominant, but there were many people who disagreed with this course of action. Many Texans who sought to fight for the Confederacy, rode to other Southern states where the fighting was. Texas had a two-fold problem of protecting a long frontier, and of raising men for service in theaters of war to the east.

It is impossible to determine the exact number of Texans who were in military service. Fifty to sixty thousand may be a conservative estimate.

The main impact of the war on Texas livelihood was a drastic reduction in exports as the Union Navy blockaded the coastal ports. While times were hard, Texas suffered less than others in the Confederacy because the border to Mexico remained open throughout the war.

Reconstruction was a galling experience for Texans who found themselves the conquered rather than the conquerors. Increased control by the Federal Government did not set well and it is clear in retrospect that officials in Washington did not understand the desire of Texans for independence and their strong distaste for governmental intervention in their lives. While there was very little slave ownership in Texas, the abolishment of slavery complicated cultural adjustment adding to the turmoil. Reconstruction was the era of "Radical Republicanism" when those who had opposed secession had their day for retaliation. As to be expected, such adjustments were conducive to violence.

THE BALLAD OF OLD INDIANOLA

[*An early Texas seaport, destroyed by a hurricane on September 17, 1875*]

O the winds blow north and the winds blow south
and the winds blow east and west,
but the winds that sigh in a dead man's sky
are winds that never rest.

The old Karankahuas are gone,
the Frenchmen come no more,
the Early Texas Pioneers
have vanished from this shore.

Their sailing ships have sailed away,
their rails, rusting in sand,
no longer carry immigrants
across a promised land.

The creaking stage and Wells–Fargo
that hurried down these roads,
now come and go in dead men's dreams
bearing their ghostly loads.

O the winds blow north and the winds blow south
and the winds blow east and west,
but the winds that sigh in a dead man's sky
are winds that never rest.

Too late the raging tides went down
and screaming winds found rest;
too late the ancient sun arose
and traveled toward the west

to look upon the tumbled heaps
of wood and stone and flora
and all the silent, swelling flesh
that once was Indianola.

O the winds blow north and the winds blow south
and the winds blow east and west,
but the winds that sigh in a dead man's sky
are winds that never rest.

James M. Thomas

A WOUNDED GIANT

[January 28, 1861]

Governor Sam Houston shifts his large frame,
and extends his San Jacinto leg to ease his pain,
the ever-present pain of twenty-five years.

At San Jacinto in '36, as he spurred horse and men,
he had felt no pain as his boot filled with blood
until after Santa Anna's men cowered in defeat;
only then was he lifted from his horse.

But today, pain is two-pronged as the battle of words
is fought to accept or defeat the "Ordinance of Secession"
to take Sam Houston's Texas from the Union.
Each *Yes* vote is a cannonball to his chest;
blood rushes to his face with each *Yes,* then recedes
to leave him ashen, and his giant's heart aching.

One hundred sixty-seven times he winces,
drawing little comfort from seven *No* votes of supporters.
Texas, not as old as a state as a boy of voting age,
starts packing to leave his home, and his *father.*

A fog of insurgency has rolled in, dimming,
or obscuring the memory of San Jacinto,
hiding the memory of Texas's birth pangs,
and the growing pains as an adolescent nation.
One hundred sixty-seven delegates refusing
to peer deeply enough into the fog to see
the achievements of its two-time President, Sam Houston:
the forging of a nation, the welding of Texas to the Union,
the pleading for Texas as its senator, its governor.

January 28, 1861, one of Texas's last giants starts dying.

March 16, 1861

The grave moves closer to Sam Houston
as the governor's mantle is stripped from him;
a mantle to be retained by renouncing his oath,
his sacred oath of allegiance to the Union,
a mantle to be retained if he swears
for the Confederacy.

Sam Houston's hand-hewn cane sounds taps as he leaves
the Governor's office, a wounded giant, never to return.

Jack E. Murphy

1862

A CITY BESIEGED

[*Galveston, October–December, 1862*]

Leaving San Augustine, we felt the sun set
in hot melts on our backs, the same searing fire
we set our watches to this morning 200 miles back
in a tide-swept graveyard in Galveston.
We had come down from the deep, cool and fatherly
forests of the whippoorwill, out to ride
the fervent litanies of Texas. Caught up
in the mysteries of its many faces, we came suddenly
to a time forgotten, a page turned backward
in history to the siege of a gallant city.

We walked there among leaning stones or no stones
to recapture our ancestors on rubbed paper:

ISAAC McCLENDON, *Beloved Husband and Father . . .*
JONAS HUNTER, *In Valiant Service, 1862 . . .*

They surfaced from cold stone crosses, these
brave men under Cook's Confederate command,
skeletal in the blast flare of thirty-two pounders,
fearfully alone in one-gun forts. Men who struggled
Christmas Day-long at Kuhn's Wharf and lost,
their womenfolks in ponder chambers sewing,
spinning, knitting uniforms to warm their volunteers.

As wordless as their sparse worded markers,
we reached out to encompass them in our arms
and cradle them like innocents, whose deeds
had not mind-touched our turbulent lives
these many years.

We had not known our fathers, then, as noble,
whose postures stood Lincolnesque in that vast
darkness, or what worth we really owned.
Or that, through the long years' toll, their truths
would emerge again, embedded in the deep mirror
of a nation's eyes. We had not come this way
in search of the foreign, forgotten landscape
of our beginnings.

Evelyn Corry Appelbee

THE BATTLE FLAG AT SABINE PASS

September 1863
At the battle of Sabine Pass
A Confederate battery
Of only forty-seven men
Commanded by Richard Dowling
Forced four thousand Union soldiers
To withdraw.

A dying Confederate soldier
Lay in blood from his wounded side
The Texas battle flag unfurled
He spoke these words before he died!

"Our Confederate flag flies high
A beautiful sight to behold
Thirteen white stars on arms of blue
White trimmed on red canton so bold!

Our Confederate flag is placed
On a stainless field of pure white
Proudly carried into battle
To honor men who bravely fight."

The soldier continued, "The blue is the sky.
Red is blood spilled on Texas sod.
Pure white is to cleanse all our souls.
The stars . . . come from God!"

Esther Mtr. Caulkins

1864

RED RIVER

Farewell, my love, you must ride to Red River
To defend our Texas domain.
I give you this ribbon. Wear it ever
Till you come to kiss me again.
    Hie you away, but do not stay;
    Come to kiss me again.

Your coat will be Gray, your brother's be Blue,
And I pray you twain will not meet.
For your mother's heart will break twice if you do,
And my joy be never complete.
    Hasten to go, but bring me no woe;
    Come to kiss me again.

You've taken a musket and left one for me
Lest Indians our home-fort overrun.
While General Dick Taylor will be glad to see
You, gone, gone is my sun.
    Let General Banks know a victorious foe;
    Come to kiss me again.

Return, my love, return from Red River;
Come home to our far Texas plain.
My heart will ache, my heart will quiver
Till you come to kiss me again.
    Come from those bands on war-torn sands;
    Come to kiss me again.

Nova Schubert Bair

MORNING, JUNE 20, 1865

We was watching the special troops come in,
the 114th Ohio and the Thirty-fourth Iowa,
up from Galveston Station.
I was with my brother, Bud Lee Cotton,
and this nigger come by,
helpin' the Union troops.
He was pushin' back the crowd
like a white man drunk
and he kind of jostled Bud Lee,
who wasn't going nowhere.
"Get back," he says.
"Son'bitch," Bud Lee says,
and pulls out his gun.
The nigger, he's quick as Johnson weed,
he hauls up a brickbat
ready to smash.
Bud Lee fires his pistol in the air.
The regiment pushed in,
men who had bacon for breakfast.
All them blue uniforms without no holes,
not tore-up enough for ourn,
guns too new-bright for ourn.
I put my Bowie knife through the nigger's throat.

They let me go in the morning.

Jacqueline Simon

GOODNIGHT–LOVING TRAIL

Harsh swirling clouds of prairie dust hang low
To loop the Texas longhorn's stiletto
As Goodnight herds crush beds of prickly pear
That dot the endless plains relentless flow.
With cows and calves from army fare,
The Texans drive toward Pecos, well aware
That passage through "graveyard of cowman's dreams"
Could cripple herd, till hope turns to despair.

There is no songbird trill, no cougar scream,
Where silent trails lead down to quicksand stream;
Goodnight and Loving plan each small detail,
And handshake binds agreement to be team.

As Goodnight gathers Texas herds for sale,
His partner blazes route of Loving Trail.

Marianne McFarland McNeil

ONE-EIGHT-SIX-SEVEN
[*Carpetbag Blues*]

Sam Houston's dead for four years now;
Colonel Terry purt near six.
They're yellin' acrost a blue/gray line
about who caused this fix.

There's a Union Man in Austin now;
run the Governor out on a rail.
Money in my pocket spends like time;
won't buy hammer, won't buy nail.

Heard Ole Houston stumpin' once;
scared me nigh to death.
He said this here Secession's
gonna bring down Yankee wrath.
Wasn't many could speak like that;
least not get away.
A few was lynched for talkin' the same;
least that's what they say.
Houston City's Federal Mayor
says he's Carpetbag King.
How much help you're gonna get
depends on the green you bring.

Ole Houston musta seen this time
in a real clear light.
We wouldn't a been the losers
if we hadn't joined the fight.

Guess we're gonna survive this thing;
just gotta struggle on.
We shoulda listened to Houston
before he was dead and gone.

Kirby David Sanders

RECONSTRUCTING TEXAS
[in the *Northern Standard*]

The *Northern Standard* of Red River County reports that a
"battered Confederate" is passing through Nashville on his way to
Texas and lists his wounds:
first — wounded in one foot
then — shot in the arm
next — the arm completely shot off
then shot in the eye — demolished
grazed in the abdomen by a minié rifle — causing
"entrails to drop nearly to his knees"
frostbitten in West Virginia — thereby losing
three toes on his left foot

In Washington, impeachment hearings.
In Austin, a convention to reconstitute the state.
In the *Northern Standard* John Mitchell warns that
"this General Grant, whether drunk or sober,
is unhappily a blockhead."

Print columns bulge with bankruptcy notices
and the newspaper itself sells bankruptcy forms.
Boys are warned against bone-softening tobacco
and young ladies against fashionable imported
hairpieces, taken from the bodies of the dead.
"Be prepared also for the worms" — an adversary
"who does not often send his armies upon you in this
latitude." But, "if you discern the fly,
make small bright fires through the fields at night."

Grown men gather to play marbles because it is
dull, they say, in Clarksville.
Others test whether "a tallow candle, fired from an
ordinary gun with the usual charge of
powder at a deal board three quarters of
an inch thick will pass through the board."

Black men vote for the first time in Texas,
and the *Almanac* concludes from experimental
evidence that yes, white men can pick cotton
in the sun and live.

Betty S. Flowers

BUFFALO SOLDIER

[*Buffalo soldier, a title of respect bestowed by Indian warriors on Negro cavalrymen*]

The red man calls me buffalo soldier.
I used to laugh 'bout that,
'specially when I learned
they was talkin' 'bout my hair
bein' so much like the buffalo's.
To tell the truth, I'm proud
'cause Indians respect the critter.
Us black folks don't get much respect.
We tryin' hard though,
and the army is helpin' us,
'specially here on the Concho.
Settlers wouldn't be here
if it wasn't for us black soldiers
keepin' the reds away.
Course I think reds belong here;
it's the red-necks that don't.
Them crackers don't treat us good,
even though we always savin' their bacon.

They called me sucker when I was born,
from a union on a southern plantation.
I was a planned baby,
my daddy a six foot field worker
and my mama a pretty mulatto.
They called me boy when me
and the field boss' son
left my mama's breast.
Then they called me nigger
when I beat that boy
for rapin' my little sister.
That's when I run off out to here
But, they still call me nigger
even when I come back bleedin'
from savin' 'em.

Maybe one of these days
they'll see the blood
past the black skin
and know that I'm a man.

Opie R. Houston

1870

SUNRISE, AUGUST 26, 1870

"Three men are here. I see them, Henry, near the gate
outside," Amanda Kelly whispered to her husband. "Two
we know are wearing hats pulled down on their faces . . .
the other one's a stranger. They're on their horses
and too quiet. I don't like it, Henry. Please
don't let them cause us trouble."

Honest Dewitt County Texan, young Kelly walked to the door.
One man spoke. "Step outside. We want to talk with you.
We want you to go with us to Hallettsville." "Well,
my horse is out; I'll have to drive him up." "Take my mule."
That was Doc White speaking; then to his pal, John Meador,
"You go and help him." Henry turned and went inside
to fetch his gun and holster. "No need to take that
six-shooter. You're a prisoner. Simmons here's
with the State Police; he lives in Hallettsville,
and he's been sent for you and your brother William."

Amanda wept as Henry changed his clothes. She brought
the fresh-ironed homespun shirt, the pants she'd washed
by hand just yesterday; and as she held these things,
she felt some mighty premonition shake her soul.
"They mean to harm you, darling, and William too.
They'll leave from here and get your brother — and why,
I'd like to know. That new Governor Davis
is behind it. Reconstruction, hah!"

"Now Mandy, don't you worry! I'm innocent of any crime."

"But Henry, I'm afraid. They say the State Police don't mind
to murder in the name of E. J. Davis, that Texan-hater-
dictator who's put himself in office to get revenge."

Amanda reached the hilltop then to watch. The men
were in a clearing, closed in by thick bushes. They talked
and Sutton raised his gun and fired. William, loading
his pipe, sank to the ground. Another shot rang out.
Henry fell from his horse. Again and again White and Sutton
fired on those two bodies smoldering in dust and smoke.
Amanda screamed and ran in anguish toward the scene.
The killers disappeared into the brush.

Margie Kirkland

REDEMPTION TO COME

Governor Davis, Governor Davis, champion of free schools — poor man —
Of equal rights and the rule of law, had won in '69
The Democrats said with votes of mean whites and ignorant Negroes,
By '71 abandoned by some of his own
Prudent Republicans, was gambling on a wave of immigrants —
There were sixty thousand that year, but most from the South,
Confederate veterans or their sons — to douse the land
With revenue, and with cotton prices down, was losing.

In the special elections Republican failure foretold
What the Democrats called Redemption to Come. Galveston
Perhaps led but Waco and Dallas were seething with talk
Of a tax revolt. The *ad valorem* rate
Had jumped from fifteen cents on the hundred dollars
To two dollars and a half: "The cow which furnishes
His babe with milk will soon be sold for a song."
Outraged taxpayers converged on Austin in September.

Who cherished Davis's dreams? He could say,
"I gave you free schools, protected the frontiers from marauders."
Citizens saw the cannon guarding the Capitol grounds
And trained weapons of their own at the "ruinous, unconstitutional"
one per cent
School building tax. They would remember hating Radical Reconstruction,
Would remember the cold sleety winter of '71
When the great cattle drives peaked and the market collapsed,
With Redemption would lower the taxes but keep the schools.

And the sixty thousand immigrants with more and many more to follow
came with greening dreams as to a court of last
Resort, some boldly inscribing their names
And records. Others scarcely made traces. They were pushing
Past the Brazos miles north of settlements,
Stopping between the Bosque and Leon to build dugouts
That would soon be replaced by proud houses aimed
At the cold or scorching wind, marking main streets.

Joseph D. Stamey

1872

POLONIS ORTIZ CONFESSING TO SERGEANT WILSON

It was no woman's life soft with milk
and easy bread to follow wagon ruts
in gathering unguarded herds, Comancheros
turned drivers of cattle across those playa plains
where clouds seem far mountains west riding
the wind black to bring cold thunder flashing
night rain, and we must hold them still,
at times among low cedar twisted dark
and wet helping block their run into
arroyos where so stupid they would stand
the cottonwood night to drown in walls of water,
but we always made them live the drive with work
leathering faces and hands until we knew
we were much men to turn Texas cattle
into money and guns, much men to see the wild
Kwahadis and Mescalero Apaches tamed
to giving horses for guns, horses for us
to ride the wagon ruts where cattle are for stealing,
for driving us once more to be much men.

Jerry Craven

SACRED HEART ACADEMY

As Autumn started to ripen the pecans
The good Sisters of St. Mary of Namur
Founded the School of the Sacred Heart
In a small rented house of four rooms in Waco,
Waco — then called the Athens of Texas.

They had left their native river, the Meuse,
The violets and lilies-of-the-valley of Belgium
For the black jack oaks, the cedar elms
And the Brazos river flowing in Texas.

They left the green meadows strewn with daisies
Where soft, sleek cows chewed contentedly
For the harsh, vast prairies
Where hardy grasses fed hardy cattle . . .
But in Spring the bluebonnets and buttercups
Emblazoned the rolling hills of Texas.

What an elixir of faith and wisdom
They brought from the vertical world of spires
To the children of the rugged and strong —
Those who were fit to conquer the spaces
Stretching to the wide heavens of Texas.

Nina M. Haas

1874

BATTLE OF ADOBE WALLS

Headlong down the red dawn galloped
Lone Wolf, Quanah Parker, Stone Calf, White Shield,
three hundred Kiowa, Cheyenne, Comanche
flinging up dust and thunder, riding
red-eyed for scalps of buffalo hunters.
But the white men, warned early, fumbled for guns
in the gray light, yelled between buildings, above the boom
of a thousand hooves, black racket of war whoops,
gun butts battering the trading post doors.

Yet noon came, and nightfall, and corpse
after corpse. Ishatai's charm,
warpaint he said would turn bullets,
was a bad joke: the buffalo guns
spat death a half mile. Lone Wolf,
hair still docked to mourn his son,
watched other men's sons slung down to death.

The third day, squinting through heat,
Billy Dixon even made sport. "A scratch shot, boys!
Them Indians are most of a mile away! "
Dixon's Sharps 50 flung slugs in a flat arc,
killed two hundred buffalo a week
but not at this range. Still,
when the rifle roared and they waited open-mouthed,
the bullet hit: a warrior jerked backward,
rolled off his horse, falling from the world.
He sopped the dirt red, his ears buzzing with death
and the white men's faint whoops and hurrahs.

The warriors who lived to be penned on the reservation
could tell their children, "The buffalo
would stretch to the edge of sky. Such a herd
took all day to run past." The buffalo were gone
in four years. Even the white men had to turn
barkeeps, marshals, ranchers,
staking the plains down with towns and fences.
Billy Dixon's widow last gazed at the land
from a motorcar.

Chris Willerton

1875

QUANAH'S SUMMER OF DESPAIR

Spirit of Nocona, father of my boyhood,
forgive me, for I can no longer stand
against the white man's power.
I can no longer see my beloved people
haggard and hopeless, weary from walking,
our ponies slaughtered in Palo Duro.

Even the children, those who have lived
through winter of The Wrinkled Hand Chase,
sit quiet on the prairie.
No more games of Run-Deer-Run
for these hungry ones.

I must leave my last camp
on the Double Mountain Fork
and lead my Kwahadis from these vast plains
to the crowded reservation.
I, Quanah, would die first —
die a free and defiant brave —
but all look to me
for food and tepees and robes
where buffalo are no more.

O Spirit of my father, help me to say farewell.
Help me to be a proud and trusted
leader of my people.
As you taught my captive mother,
golden-haired Naduah,
the ways of Comanche,
teach me, her son,
to walk the white man's road.

Pauline Durrett Robertson

III
Hide, Horn And Cotton 1876–1899

As the population of Texas grew steadily, settlements moved west of the ninety-eighth meridian into the hunting grounds of the Comanche Indians who bitterly resisted this encroachment. Comanche warriors, giving no quarter nor asking quarter, fought a losing battle with the Army. The burden fell in part on the Cavalry operating in Texas. The Negro troopers involved earned the *sobriquet* of Buffalo Soldier, bestowed as a title of respect by the Indian warriors. The fighting required to confine the Indians to their reservations may be measured by the fourteen Medals of Honor awarded to these soldiers.

Eastern cities developed a taste for fresh beef, thus creating an explosive growth of the cattle industry on the Western plains. Large herds were driven to Kansas and Missouri where they were shipped by rail to Eastern stockyards. Sheep were grown for their fleece rather than for their meat, and a century would elapse before a true Texan would eat mutton with the zest reserved for chicken fried steak. By 1900, the Western frontier in Texas had moved to the state line.

Agriculture in East Texas had evolved into commercial farming of cotton and grain for export. It was subsidiary to the industrialized Eastern and Northern states, and was dependent upon Eastern financial resources. The farmer had no control over the middleman or transportation since the railroads were controlled by out of state owners. Prices were low and there was little profit. Consequently, there was dissatisfaction among the farmers leading to the rise of populism: a political philosophy which sought to reform the abuses of industrialization and to preserve the agrarian culture.

At the end of the nineteenth century, four out of five people lived in rural areas with uncertainty as to where Texas was headed: toward an industrial society, or to remain an agrarian society.

THEY WERE THE PROUD ONES

They were the proud ones,
The wild and uncowed ones;
Their hooves shook the earth as they raced
    on the plains.
They winnowed the wind for the spread scent,
    the dread scent
Of man, with his ropes, his bridles and reins.

And all through the wide land,
The western, untried land
They snorted defiance from canyons and brakes;
But slowly the vast herds, the stallion-led
    fast herds
Yielded their freedom to corrals and to stakes.

Now only a scant few,
A barely extant few
Elude cunning hunters that slaughter wholesale.
No more shall the wasteland, the wide-sweeping
    chaste land
Know the proud mustangs that once roamed its trails.

Pauline Crittenden

PHILADELPHY'S A FUR PIECE

[*The hero is commonly the simplest and obscurest of men.*
— *Thoreau*]

So y' see, ma'am, it all come up becuz I'd helpt 'em clean Santy Anna's plow in '36 an' agin at Buny Vista. We wuz t' ride th' train free f'r nuthin' plum t' this-yere sen-ten-yell in Philadelphy, they sez, an' it took in me. Didn't much cotton t' th' notion but daughter an' kids jabbered an' jawed at me till I said aw well I'd go jist t' git 'em outa m' hair, whut thur iz uv it.

Well, daughter packed me up m' vittles an' they had drinkin'-water on th' train, but wuz shy on coffee. Nights, we madc Baptist pallets on th' floor, an' I s'pose y' might say th' trip wuz fair t' middlin' with mebbe a few slouchy patches. God's plenty t' see, never fear. We rumbled over th' Miss-sippi jist when th' sun come up, an' purty soon wuz gee-in' an' hawin' up an' down them mountins an' through th' shinnery, a-ziggin' an' a-zaggin' till we rolled inta Philadelphy.

Take too much t' tell y' 'bout th' boardin'house an' noisy streets an' purtied-up big bildins at th' fairgrounds. Sorta foreintended we'd be thur th' Fourth a' July, I guess, which we wuz, an' y' never hears s' much *whoop-ti-doo* speechifyin'. Our number two chief Mister Hubbard talked f'r Texas, an' Lord help us, ma'am, he laid it on thick: reckon he musta bin fetched up someplace in Texas I never see n'r hear tell uv. He come down an' shuck hands after th' speechifyin' wuz over an' wished us a good trip home.

Well, thur wuz a ol' bearded feller showed up too: looked oldern' I am, which iz purty well along. Name a' Whitman: a poet, somebody tol' me, later on. Shuck hands all round an' said he rec'lected readin' the papers 'bout San Jacinto battle an' had wrote somethin' 'bout Goliad, I dunno jist what. Leastwise, seems he figgered we wuz somethin' extryordinary. I ain't never had much truck with poets but he 'peared a lot home-folksier'n I'd expect a poet t' be.

Comin' back wuzn't near's gaudy's goin' but with plenty t' gab 'bout time passed quick excep' track-trouble held us up so's we got back t' Austin long past midnight an' would you b'lieve it, they had a brass band an' doughnuts'n-coffee all round at that time a-night. Alwus did say Austin's a friendly kind a place.

Joseph Jones

1877

FORT WORTH

The man came from the barn. His chores were done.
The evening sun stained windows on the west.
It's been a quarrelsome year, this year
he mused, then let his thoughts go frolicking about.
The spring, the fall, with summer added in
has been the kind of year I won't forget.
A lot of changes coming down this way.
The railroad helped it come or come to be.
This side of town still has the stagecoach though.
They've stretched the line to everywhere, I hear—
to some Arizona place I never knew.

My cattle were all tethered from free range.
I "posted" thirty days and they were mine.
Wild as the wind and stronger than a storm.
It took a lot of strength to bring them in.
Now, Sarah did her part. She wasn't strong,
but she could work a day until it's done.
The time our cows went dry, we missed the milk
and out she went and brought new calves to pen.
Of course, the mother cows would show themselves,
and standing by, we milked enough to do.
When we had milk, I marked each calf to match
their mother's brand and turned them back to stray.

One morning our cows were caught into
a herd that traveled north on Chisholm Trail.
It was midmorning when I saddled up,
but riding hard I caught them bedded down.
By daylight, herdsmen helped me cut them out,
and driving back was night in getting home.
I heard, before they even came in sight,
the bawl of hungry calves with two nights gone.
Two days away can change a person's mind.
When coming back you see the land a different way.
You count the crops and what you have in store,
and wonder why the year has bothered you.
Like Sarah always said . . . come spring again, we'll see.

Mary Stallard McGaughy

JULY 21, 1878

Like vultures circling their prey, the people gathered.
They crowded the hotel, slept on floors and porches,
or walked the dusty, heat-heavy streets of Round Rock, Texas.
All waited for a man to die.

Sam Bass lay on a cot, bleeding from bullet wounds.
Already a legend, Sam was a favorite of the people.
He was no killer; instead, he was an outlaw chieftain,
dashing, courageous, generous with the money
stolen from stagecoaches, trains, and banks.
Now the people had come to share in the legend of dying,
to be able to tell their children and grandchildren,
"I was there when he died!"

Even the lawmen liked him,
until the brunt of criticism
forced them to post the reward signs:
SAM BASS . . . WANTED: DEAD OR ALIVE.
Headquartered at Denton,
he eluded the lawmen from Galveston to the Panhandle.
"Sam Bass is harder to catch than a greased owl,"
one posse member said, and it was true.
Moving at night, circling, Sam led the lawmen
over rocky terrain, through woods, across creeks
and into swamp or brush-tangled ravines named Cove Hollow,
Hickory Branch Bottom, Pilot Knob, Big Caddo, Salt Creek.

Although betrayed by a member of his gang,
in his dying hours, Sam would not betray any of his men.
Instead, he said, "If a man knows anything important,
he oughta die with it in him,"
and he did at two minutes before four o'clock, July 21, 1878,
on his twenty-seventh birthday.

Pat Stodghill

SHANNON DONEGAL

[*The Story of Shannon Donegal, A Composite Hero*]

I remember that day in November
earlier, in the embers of my campfire
above Dexter where I had killed a timber

wolf. I saw the fact of my life, a dire
future if judged from where I'd been
I knew a kinship with the wolf when

I saw him fall: gambler and misfit
So I crossed the Red and rode with a bit
of new luck into Gainesville. Was it sin

or chance that brought me to the railroad
just as a loud crowd with streamers
flags and brass bands brought the first load

of passengers, freight and new dreamers
into town. It was then I saw the end
of my wandering, the vision and the friend

who was to lead me, my beautiful winning streak
That night I sold my horse and saddle, too weak
to ride away from love. Chose her as my end

or a new beginning. So that blonde at last
was the luck that kept me winning there
The pot that night: the insurance against my past

led me into the swirl of social life and fair
glory, a carriage of gold with glass doors
and fast horses, high halls and dance floors.

I remember in 1884 for the Cattleman's Ball
her $1500 gown from Paris took the breath of all
her beauty, her style. Nothing this side the shores

of Paradise could have made me leave my ways
except that woman, the angel and the chorister
of what became my Victorian dream: our days

grew into one long day. So through a mixture
of faith and luck that lone wolf at Dexter
led me here. I've seen the town fulfill

its destiny and mine, seen it refine
the fortunes of many beside hers and mine
here in Gainesville where I found my will.

Joseph Colin Murphey

MUSEUM PIECE

[*The Indian could not live without the buffalo for food, shelter and clothing. The extinction of the buffalo forced them to reservation living.*]

Texas historical museum.
Father and son visiting it.
Mural in Texas room.
Almost could by one step enter —
Be a part of
As an actor in it:

Cowboy of West Texas
Sitting tall on wiry mustang,
Eyes toward far horizon
Dusty with storm driven band
Tattooing hooves on baked ground,
Tails toward the wind,
Heads lowered in onrush.

Blue glint of cowboys' eyes,
Hand on coiled lariat,
Ready to pull the rein and plunge
To turn the compact mass
Of living flesh.

Opposite, but almost mirroring cowboy,
Indian on shriveled pony
Views the same scene.
Shoulders slumped, dispirited,
Moccasins, tattered,
Buckskin trousers, worn;
No bow and arrow,
No spear in hand, no feathers or beads,
Silently he waits.
In front, balancing the herd,
One gleaming white, dried skull
Of buffalo, bleached to chalkiness.
"What does the painting mean, Father?
". . . the storm, the cattle, the skull?"

"They call it Progress, Son. Progress."

Mary Walker Beamer

1881

MEETING THE WIRE

[*In 1881, barbed wire was introduced in Texas.*]

The wire: I saw it shine before heat and cold burned it brown. Saw it barbed, like those who fought the plains while I tried to hustle out an outlaw's golden yarn to sell. But I drifted away from hope for fame. I watched the new fence rise. It came from the North where defeat had come from — my family's home in Taladega (Alabama) gone to Sherman's wanton flames, and my brother lost, I never knew where he was, and my first son killed in a fight, my wife disappearing in bedlam in New Orleans. All I found in my journey was grief and wire and the knowledge that my sun, a fractured confederacy of dreams, was setting.

Riding northwest after a mill I built burned down in the east Texas pines, I came to open rolling land. Built houses in Seymour, and took a new wife. Her honeyed stream of endless talk brought neighbors to our porch in the evening when scissortails agitated hawks in the cloud-mountained sky.

The wire, though, ripped my pants and shirt, nicked blood from my skin, and the urge for a tale of a pearl-pistoled outlaw came back, came back and fled. I did have a yarn, but all I wanted to say was that wire was the wind, the hot chapping wind scorching my green eyes pale. I wanted to say that the wire was the mill I built that was doomed, that thorns hooked the wire and the world, but my wife softened those points, and we had then a son, yet I was still tangled.

From the heartless north, blue wind was singing a hard winter in, but my fine-talking wife rolled another sweet pressure against me. The business, though, went bust, and we left this place, rolled in a wagon northeast toward the Red River whose clay-thick flow became the blood in our flesh.

The wire: I saw it plot the land with a babel of tongues and trouble, but the cool dry nights felt light, my son's young talk as honeyed as his mother's, though his mouth moved as rarely as mine. The stars had patterns I forgot how to name, and my heart was on fire, my craw burned raw. The huge sky was falling into an ocean of dust, but my wife was the talker, not I. I kept my own bad news to myself.

James Hoggard

GRAMPA'S IRON HORSES

[1882 — Marshall and Northwestern Railroad established. Rio Grande and Pecos Railroad founded. Galveston, Sabine and St. Louis Railroad Company chartered.]

Whenever I cross a train track, it plays, in memory
like a favorite record, one of Grampa's yarns about
the railroads. I can almost hear his raspy twang . . .

"Yes siree, boy, they wuz sumpin' ta see — When the wild west
was won and railroads had thur day,
when the stillness of the buffalo grass was furst broke
by the roar of pistons, and th' sounds of *clickety-clack,*
when rumble came upon the ground like wild stampedes on
yonder hills n' plains.

Year of '82 it wuz, an' me jist a whippersnapper, nairy bit
older 'n you now. Y'see, we knowed sumpin' wuz a-comin'
when they put down them arn rails. Why, my eyes bulged wide
as a bullfrog.

An' then they come! Like stampedes of arn hosses on metal
clad trails roamin' where only the deer, antelope, and buffalo
once know'd, on tracks crisscrossin' th' countryside like
patches on Grandma's quilt. Whistles screechin', steam a-hissin',
a-roarin' n' a-puffin' like a black arn monster — Scatterin'
hosses n' cattle n' folks like th' Devil hissef!
An' they jist kep a-comin', more n' more ev'ryday.
Like 'em big snakes, they wrapped thur coils 'round nature's
four-legged critters and, in due time, swallowered 'em up."

Looking around, I'd say, "So many of them! But where'd they
all go to, Grampa? " Then he'd lean back in the porch swing,
eyes half closed, and sigh, "Same place they come out of,
I reckon — hist'ry, that is. Out run by cars n' trucks, same
as they outrun th' hosses. Anserin' ta one law. Th' one thing
we kin all count on, boy. Only thing that stays the same in
eny hist'ry."

"What's that, Grampa?"
"Change itsef, boy. Change."

Jerry C. Elliott

Best Wishes! Jerry Elliott

1883

"OXCART JOHN" — THE LENGTH OF LEADERSHIP

In retrospect
John Ireland was moon-rocket wise in a frontier era.
Experienced as a delegate to the Secession Convention and
Constitutional Congress
He commanded with authority as Governor 1882 to 1887
A time when fires of war had died and scarce was the memory —
a time when Texas was restless with men moving west
milling masses poured over state lines
remanent carpetbaggers plied their wiles
and vexing fence wars erupted with guns used as law!

"Too conservative, returning to oxcart ways"
Were accusations from railroad barons and pork-barrel peddlers
But not a vassal for anyone, his vision was nobler than theirs —
A vision that considered the children's children
And so he ordered investment of school funds in 6% bonds
and forbade sale of any more school land at 50¢ per acre!

To the railroad's grab for more free land, he said *No*
And *No* to those wanting Indiana stone for the new State Capitol.
He purchased Burnet red granite — 45 miles away
"Good Texas stone for our Capitol" said he
And a splendid statehouse is a monument to his unwavering will.
His march for merit enduring as the stone!

Whether pulled by lobbyists or legislators,
He plucked his own lyre and sang his own song
Authoring laws to protect State lands
and protect citizens from criminals.
Those seeds of wise decisions planted then are today's harvest.

We recall John Ireland's foresight —
His part in the growing of greatness, fleshing out Texas with his firmness
And the derisive label, "Oxcart John" became a title of respect.

The length of his leadership still stretches across Texas!

Shirley Jones Handley

ELEANORA IN EL PASO

Mrs. Chatham bustles past the window
toward home to end an afternoon of shopping,
and the Fincher boys, toting
feed in their hand-pulled, slatted wagon,
and Mrs. Johnson's maid, hurrying on some errand —
to buy a ham hock, maybe, for the white beans;
then a pair of lovers moving toward the sunset
pauses by her window. They can't see,
the lamp unlighted, behind the eyelet curtain.
He picks a rose that leans beyond the picket fence
and threads his sweetheart's bodice
with vermilion stain.

He left the church alone. I followed,
telling Mother of a message for Mrs. Parker —
that I would presently be home.
He stood by a mulberry tree
near Baxter's road, I behind nandina
until she came.
When they touched, sight blurred.
The doctor said that vapors sent me
to my bed; then weeks of fever came.

In the low lamplight Eleanora neatly
lays aside her clothes, washes
in the porcelain bowl, then, seated at her mirror,
unbinds her brown and graying hair.
Gaze fixed upon herself, she traces
with her hand the length of hair across her breast.
She lifts a flower from the vase
and lies, eyes closed, her heart beneath the rose.
One by one she pulls the petals free, bruising
between her fingers their velvet mold.
Fading, Eleanora
slowly rubs the pungent folds again,
again across her lips,
her nose.

Lynn Novak

BIG SPREAD — XIT

Cheers ripped the air on second March, 1885
As cornerstone of new capitol was hoisted in place.
Between hurrahs, Texans smirked, "Pulled a sharp
One on those Yankees, the finest for some no count land."
Builders surprised, had to build railroad, buy oxen
To move the Texas granite as required, cost had overrun
Half a million, would take a million more to clear the title.

Sight unseen the Chicagoans had bought a dream —
Three million acres of treeless plains would bloom;
could never comprehend their water woes, so sure
Artesian bores would cure. All unheeding they ordered
"Enclose in barbed wire," overlooked lack of posts.
"Hurry, hurry, buy longhorns," twenty-two thousand
In scattered herds plodding a wavering line across seared
Plains headed two hundred miles north to Buffalo Springs.
Horns clicked, cattle snorted, heifers bawled,
Moving in rhythm when not crazed by thirst.

Ab Blocker, who'd sighted the North Star
Down the backs of more longhorn steers than any other
Determined to be first to put cattle on the Big Spread,
Pushed his herd through the night to beat rivals.
As day broke, cattle scented water, raised heads and tails,
Snorted and clattered down the slope to source.
"No brand? Hell you ain't got a ranch till you got a brand,"
Blocker said, stooped down, began to doodle in the dust.
Soon came up with XIT. "Simple to apply, hard to change."
Others said "Ten in Texas," but there were only nine.

Housing, fencing, cattle, railroads and Capitol building —
Money ran short, led to British Syndicate. British didn't
Know the price was high and odds poor. Thus the biggest
Ranch began to operate, where anything could happen,
Anywhere, anytime except water in Taylor's artesian wells —
Dogged by water shortage, blizzards, jealous neighbors,
Fires that swept across thousands of acres in a night,
Falling market and orders from the city where all they knew
About a cow was Mrs. O'Leary's.

Farwell's dream of cropland was premature, it took
Advent of strong pumps to tap underground water.
Thumbnail sketch of XIT — big sky, space, windmills,
Pond water, range horses in rope corrals and TROUBLE.
Swallower of lives, of dedicated men, almost none
Survived to see the eventual blooming.

Evelyn McDaniel Morris

1886

YOUNG COWBOY TO OLD-TIMER

Not one man knew what would befall
Long days ago when West was young.
Old-Timer, what do you recall?

Crossing prairies to cattle's bawl
With slicker and rope saddle-slung,
Not one man knew what would befall.

Rough rivers caused crazed cattle-stall
Which cowboys had to ride among.
Old-Timer, what do you recall

Of evening camp, lighthearted brawl,
As song to a guitar was sung?
Not one man knew what would befall

When answering adventure's call
To cattle kingdoms, rich, far-flung.
Old-Timer, what do you recall?

Does all seem lost in caterwaul
Of towns and cities from prairie sprung?
Not one man knew what would befall.
Old-Timer, what do you recall?

Margaret F. Scott

THE GREAT DROUGHT

All summer had the drought hung on.
Before the corn could ear,
Before the milo maize could yield,
The stalks stood stark and sere.

No fodder now for starving stock —
The grazing grass lay dead,
And troubled cowmen wondered how
Their cattle could be fed.

Persistent sun had drained the ponds,
The creekbeds stood bone-dry,
And helpless ranchers cringed to watch
Their thirsting cattle die.

Always before whenever need
Or sickness plagued another,
The neighboring men would pool their all
To help a stricken brother.

But now they shared a common lot —
No one could beg or barter —
For everyone for miles about
Knew scarcity of water.

The level of long-trusted wells
Had sunk through months of drought
Till no one dared to drink a drop
That he could do without.

Strong men grew faint on seeing herds,
Near prostrate from the heat,
Seek refuge from the blazing sun
Beneath a lone mesquite.

And ranchers wincing openly
At every anguished moo,
Drew water from their scanty store.
What further could they do?

Than pray and wait the anodyne
Ordained for such a sorrow —
The blessed anodyne called hope
That comes with each tomorrow.

Vivian Ricker

1888

THE NEW COWBOY

Across the fence he was mending
he saw the queue of smoke
black against the winter sky.
The Santa Fe was making its first run
to Panhandle City.

He had watched barbed wire
fence the open range
into squares of pasture;
and the coming of the trains
that carried the wire and posts
to the great new cowpens.

He would never again lie under wide sky
and sing to the herd
nor ride, with ten thousand hooves
clattering around him in stampede,
his life hanging on every sure step
of his horse.
He would never feel the wind whip him
on lonely night guards
nor dread the blizzards
that sent the cattle drifting southward
and left a thousand carcasses
frozen in the snow.
He would never again swear in winter
that he had ridden his last trail;
then find himself eager in spring
for roundup.

There would be no more roundups.

He would cut hay in the dry riverbottoms
and ride the thin world of the fence.

He whom time would lift in film and song
to legend
with the mustang and the longhorn
watched the dark tail of the train,
cursed it
and spat into the ankle-deep dung.

Marcella Siegel

1889

JULY 19, 1889. WHY THIS DAY, MATT?

Matt Ford
bellerin' Methodist, good neighbor, vigilante
you hide in Postman Turner's cotton field,
finger on trigger, as he walks behind his plow.
How did you come to this day?

Been nigh ten years since Fire-an'-Brimstone
Preacher Smith, Parson Meeks an' you
hooked up with th' San Saba County Mob.
"Necessary," you nodded. Rus'lin's gotta stop.
Law ain't doin' nothin'." That first lynchin'
remember seein' them buggin' eyes fer weeks?
Worked, though. Them that wouldn't git
shot or hung. Then good folks started talkin'
Shame t' treat 'em like crooks. Had t' stop 'em.

Why couldn' old Turner keep his mouth shet?
Tellin' that troublemaker Daughtery,
"I don't like all this killing, and Matt's in it."
Been warned, too, back in April, t' git.
Give him three days. Now July's half over.

Jus' last week you hammered nails
in a coffin fer Turner's drowned young'un,
shrugged yore humped shoulders at thanks.
Asked yore cousin, "What air kinfolks fer?"
You'd send yore boy, Jim, t' finish her plowin'

A summer storm, darkened sky. A foreshadowin'?
Two trials in Austin. Hung juries, shore
but folks ever after spittin' yore name
"Matt Ford, Bellerin' Methodist, MURDERER!

The trigger finger tightens
the shot shatters the silence.

Ovon Ross

BILLY DIXON REMEMBERS: "1890 LOOSED THE TIDE!"

[*Dixon was an Indian scout, buffalo hunter, pioneer and plainsman*]

I

"The mighty Legislature met,
(And I recollect with pride),
How they opened new land for sale
With boundaries far and wide,
Up the Llano Estacado
Where the Spanish Staked Plain spills
Down the descending escarpment
Onto raw caliche hills;
Across the cool Canadian,
The sandy waters divide
Rolling currents of the Cimarron
From No-Man's southern side
Of Oklahoma Indian Lands.
(Some said the Territory
Was only one jump from Hell, and
A skip to Purgatory!)"

II

"But some folks kept on acomin' . . .
Well, more than you ever saw!
There's three families between Rita Blanca
And Palo Duro Draw!
One above Wolf Creek and Tule;
No, there might be two, at least,
In dugouts on Goodnight's Gulley
With Turkey Track over East.
Past Bugbee and Adobe we fought
Cheyenne, Arapahoe,
Kiowa and Comanche; now lay
Lands undone by plow and hoe . . .
Sunbonnets, blooms and buffalo,
New babies on every hand:
Echo undaunted whisperings
To accommodate the land!"

III

"Yes, the Texan Legislature,
In mighty wisdom and pride,
Set free the northern lands,
And 1890 loosed the tide!"

Jenna V. Ownbey

WAR AND PEACE

PRELUDE

There is a place where water-willows mingle with mesquite
and paddle cactus overruns the hills;
where summertime is hot enough to bake a rattlesnake,
in contrast to December's ice and chills.

INTERLUDE, December 1891

I am Maria.
I belong to Don Pedro, who owns this estancia.
I work in the cantina, making tortillas and
cooking the frijoles in that big clay pot.
Don't ask me about the revolution!
Porfirio Diaz is no concern of mine:
He runs Mexico — I run this cantina!
And Catarino Garza? He lives in Texas — why, then
does he stir up rebels on both sides of the river,
raiding Texians for supplies to bring here,
making troubles for Mexico?
The Federales will get him, if the Rangers from Texas
or the U.S. Cavalry can't.

That river, you know, is just a liquid ribbon.
Men come and go; from side to side, too easy, too easy.
The cavalry comes across, and hardly gets the boots wet!
They were tracking Garza, but when they found him this time,
he didn't melt from sight into the chaparral,
Garza and his rebels surrounded them, and shot it out!

It is a shame about the young man — what's his name?
Si, Corporal Edstrom. I'm glad I have no sons!
They say he was the happy sort. I say novenas for his mother.
It must be sad for her; the end of his life, the end of the year,
And the beginning of this tinhorn war which can't be won,
Even though she lost her son.

POSTLUDE

There is a place where water-willows mingle with mesquite
And paddle cactus overruns the hills
and Garza's ghost and Edstrom's ghost
Meet in a clash of wills.

Doris K. Ferguson

WHEN TEXAS JOINED THE USA

In Texas in 1892
Did snow fall in Galveston?
Did rain flood Amarillo?
Were there three calm days in the Panhandle?
I could probably say "yes" to all three
And get by with the lie,
But I'm an honest man.

Outside of Texas in 1892, Walt Whitman died —
On the twenty-sixth of March (to be exact),
In a little house on Camden's Mickle Street,
Eight years (to the day) after he moved there,
And in the same year of the ninth edition of the *Leaves*.
He might have sung a song of Texas:

Over the plains endlessly blowing
The west wind drifts an aria
of Texas joining the USA,
Of James Stephen Hogg fighting the railroads,
Of his winning a mandate in reelection
(A real statistician's mandate),
Of Texas abandoning a line of Confederates
A quarter of a century
After the brother-against-brother battles,
And, in 1892,
Of reelecting their first native governor
As an exclamation point.
And the west wind blows toward the east.

T. J. Kallsen

1893

LONE BUGLE NOTE FROM THE BORDER

He was a rebel,
Wore a black hat in two countries
        a quarter century before Pancho.
His band hopped and skipped the Rio
Grande
        like the river changed meander.

White hats chased them on both sides
        of the border,
One, a silk top hat — rich friend to the rich —
The other, friend to that friend.
The revolutionary, sandwiched between,
        sounded a note of hope to the poor.

Two years they cat–moused: Rebels,
Mexican
        Army, Texas Rangers,
Back and forth across the river —
Mabry, north, Adjutant General,
Diaz, south, President,
Catarino Garza, Rebel, in the middle,
        directing a revolution against
        one country from another.

Sometimes revolutionaries swap hats,
        exchange black for white,
        rebel to hero.
Not this time.
Two companies of Texas Rangers ate
        the sandwich one January day
        in '93,
Silenced the lone bugle note on the border,
        called it the Tin Horn War,
        lost it in the footnotes.

Georgia Earnest Klipple

PIONEER WOMAN OF TEXAS

She survived Sherman's march through the South,
Rode the train from Missouri and Ohio,
Received her teaching certificate, boarded at a ranch.
Buttercups grew on her soddy and hollyhocks to the
outhouse —
Courageous woman, pioneer of Texas.

She came from Germany to settle where the priests led,
Drove the oxen hitched to the covered wagon from Tennessee,
Homesteaded the endless acres, and escaped the Comanche
attack.
She put on an apron, built and nurtured a generation —
Faithful woman, pioneer of Texas.

Her face masked a matriarch; traveling to cure consumption,
She assisted the doctor and midwife, survived slow fever;
She shot the deer and killed the rattlesnake,
Read the *Bible* by lamp, led the schoolchildren through
the snowstorm —
Sturdy woman, pioneer of Texas.

She ordered bone corsets from Sears catalogue,
Carded wool, knitted stockings and sewed cotton shirts,
Milked the cows, hatched little chicks, made lye soap,
Pieced quilts, rode sidesaddle on duty calls —
Diligent woman, pioneer of Texas.

She made agarita jelly, souse, and sauerkraut,
Kept chili beans hot on the stove, burned prairie chips,
Exchanged hot biscuits for a sack of cowboy's flour,
Carried water from the windmill; boiled and flatironed
clothes —
Industrious woman, pioneer of Texas.

She stood on the horizon among sandstorms and droughts
And envisioned schools and churches for her youth;
She waited for the return of her hunter or rancher
And prepared for culture, for art and for the right to vote —
Patient woman, pioneer of Texas.

Colleen Church Leonard

TIMELAND WAITS

Lemuel Clepper had toughed out the Civil War
Then roamed with the rootless another dozen years
Till MarthaLiz Griffith, somewhere off Caddo's shore —
Mid-teens wed mid-thirties — exceptional meld of careers.
Babes eight were born at Caddo, six still alive
When his life at home and on river steamers was done
And he crossed the Styx in Eighteen Ninety Five.
Where, where O where have the forbears gone!
Jim was the elder, well able to help his Mom
To bring up the brood, backed up by LemJunior, fourteen.
They lived not poor, but instead of a bank, Old Lem
Had used a cast-iron dinner pot, so unseen
And unknown, that this orphaned wherewith was never found.
Even worse, in fewer than three wan winters along
The youthful Mom joined Big Lem in the Bright Beyond.
Bless, Bless Timeland, where the families throng!

The Buffalo Soldiers had worn Victorio down
The Fort on the Conchos had finaled a peace on the Plains
So Jim and Lem went seeking the virgin ground
Where General Lee had taught his troopers the pains
Of the Red Man's rage . . . folk called it Robert Lee.
And "Cousin Ira" at Sanco, where Chief Sanaco fell
Could "show them the ropes" in a land as thorned as the tree,
Mesquite. Jim soon married, but Lem stood tall
And strict by boy Ernest and sisters three.
War makes heros, but the hero in Lem came alive
When Fate took Lem Senior in Eighteen Ninety Five.

Bless, Bless O Bless . . . Timeland, where forebears wait!

Vernon Payne

O. HENRY (William S. Porter)

His newspaper *Rolling Stone* had crumbled,
        (not so long begun,)
and First National of Austin was
        missing quite a fund.
Still, a man of words and laughter for the
        moment might delete
frowns of Federal Grand Jury, year of
        eighteen ninety-six,
when the *Houston Post* was needing such a
        fellow for their "sheet."
Some sure thought he must be guilty; he was
        in an awful fix.
Travel lured. So to New Orleans, then
        Honduras for a spell,
to forget in land of flowers and of
        music — somehow beat
haunt of trial time approaching — two years off . . .
        And then, ah well:
First short story sold and rolling!
        More to flood from New York streets!
Even prison would not shadow their bright
        immortality.
Surprise endings! William Porter
        now forever *O. Henry!*

Ruth Webber Shively

SHROUDED MEMORY

[*The Hexagon House Hotel was built in Mineral Wells, Texas, in 1897*]

The news of healing caused a prairie fire —
And pain-racked people gathered in a throng
To drink the crystals, sparkling like desire,
And bathe where mineral waters brought a song.
The town was suddenly ablaze with need
To feed and house the scores of migrants there:
Some business ventures grew from selfish greed,
While others started after fervent prayer.

The hotel with a fascinating shape
Gained legendary status overnight.
It wrapped folk in a huge, six-panel cape
And left an inner glow of candlelight.
The years destroyed that lovely work of art
And hung a shrouded memory on man's heart!

Joy Gresham Hagstrom

MUSINGS OF AN OLD RANGE RIDER

Fourteen years with that old snip-nosed Blaze,
riding the canyons, rimrocks and draws;
Or searching for strays in the thickets,
of scrubby mesquite and sharp catclaws.
Five years I spent with the one called "Sol,"
a short, rattailed, ewe-necked zebra dun;
He got his name from the way he bucked,
he'd toss you half way to the sun.

Ten years with that fiddle-footed bay,
with a gait like an old rocking chair;
He could go from morn till midnight,
trot all day, and never turn a hair.
And when it came time for spring branding,
that old bay hoss was in his glory;
his skill at cutting calves from the herd
was often told in song and story.

I loved them all, they respected me,
we worked together as a team;
As I look back on the time we shared,
a lot of it seems just like a dream.
They stayed with me thru thick and thin,
cold, blowing snow, howling wind and dust;
I'm sure they'll get their just reward,
for they all fulfilled a sacred trust.

And now, old Pal, you've served me well,
tho I'll *not* say that you were the best;
For each one did what was asked of him,
no one was better than the rest.
Now Father Time has taken his toll,
we have come to the end of our rope;
It's time for us to make way for youth,
and enjoy the things for which we hoped.

For you, old Pal, the tall, lush green grass,
no more saddle sores or thorns from brush;
You can pick your spot and graze all day,
there's nowhere to go in a big rush.
As for me, I have all I'll need,
a warm bedroll, a good frying pan;
A firelit nook where I can dream,
and live it all over again.

Thomas J. Henderson

1899

THE BRAZOS FLOOD

Today in a room in Brenham,
where the Brazos Deep Water Committee
was scheduled to meet,
a giant oak table and twelve carved chairs
knock against each other. Six feet
of muddy water
laps at the plaster walls. Tomorrow,
the Fourth of July,
promises no parades, no bands to march
the flooded streets
of Belton, Sealy, Bellville . . . every town
from Waco down to Richmond.

Outside the Bryan High School Gym,
a tuba filled with reddish silt
lies beached on a hill like a brass whale.
Weakened hands
clutch all they can save, cling to windmills,
to housetops. Tired eyes
search for trains,
cut off by washed out bridges,
search for boats,
rare in a land of farmers.

Four days ago the storm began. Some say
the wind blew harder than back in 'Seventy-Five.
Sorghum blown flat.
Corn beaten to the ground.
Bloated bodies
trapped in treetops and barbed wire fences.
Near Calvert,
where the Little Brazos joins the Big Brazos,
one Brazos, ten miles wide, rages.
The conquistadors
named it, *El Rio de los Brazos de Dios*,
The River of the Arms of God.
Today, His arms are filled.

Milt McLeod

NIGHT RAID

Without warning demonic forces devoured the land.

Uprooting the gulf, power winds manipulated
massive walls of water
thrashing coastlines
clawing defenseless shores.

Piers disappeared. Seafront houses smashed,
foundations floundered, fell
spilling, killing, in darkness.

Cut off from mainland Texas, civilization vanished.

Invading as people slept, colossal waves captured the community
rearranging lives forever
flinging families from sleep to deepest sleep.

Misery's ledger lengthened as day followed night.

Sunlight spotlighted what darkness hid
creating a vacuum of shocked survivors
viewing spewed debris of tangled matter.

Violence spent, hurricane swollen clouds
found other shores to pound,
releasing gulf waters
to return to the tide.

Galveston's islanders massed in revival to survive and
with chaos mounting, counted their dead.
Seasoaked and desolate Galveston mourned
six thousand–twelve thousand souls and more!

Irene Carmichael

IV
Oil and Industry
1900–1929

At the turn of the century, Texas was fifty years behind in the degree of industrialization attained in the Northern and Mid-Western states, because Texas was primarily rural and lacked a source of energy. The pervasive populist culture in rural Texas was hostile to industrial development, because the populists blamed capitalistic industrialization for all problems plaguing the farmer. While there was an abundance of lignite (brown coal) in Texas, it was a poor substitute for the coal found in the Northern states. Such industry as did exist was tied to the needs of the farmer.

A radical change in the availability of energy came with Spindletop in 1901, for energy became abundant through petroleum. Soon it was dominant with its associated industries of exploration, production and refining. Growth was slow due to the need for markets and to the inhibiting populist culture. But, that resistance began to diminish with the increased move of people from the farm to the city.

The growth of the petroleum industry was progressive. First came kerosene used in rural areas for cooking, light and heat. The ubiquitous five-gallon kerosene container could be found everywhere; most useful for pots and pails as well as a source of sheet tin. The Model T supplanted the horse and buggy reducing the barrier of distance and calling for gasoline rather than oats. The growth of central heating called for natural gas and heating oil. And, of course, the natural gas and fuel oil used to generate electricity provided horsepower as a substitute for manpower.

The Texas climate being well known to Army officials, one of the first Wright airplanes was sent to Fort Sam Houston for training purposes. By 1915, the first Aero Squadron was organized there, and was part of the punitive expedition organized to cope with Pancho Villa. World War I brought numerous training bases and flying fields. Many of the young men who trained in Texas remained or returned to make their homes in the state.

WIDE-EYED

We all wanted to see it when it came
to Old John, the indisputable proof
of riches.
Not so much that we had no shame
as simply, we were curious sons
of bitches.

What would he do with one hundred thousand
of what he'd been used to having at most
by tens?
He, with one Sunday pair of trousers,
a two-room box, a row of collards,
and nine hens?

Oil in Kilgore, all we slaved to squeeze,
flowed no more steady than the sense
in Old John's head.
What should he know of royalties?
Well, first he'd have a gentleman's talk
with Mistah Ledd.

If the signs was right, then he proposed
going over to Shreesport and buy the biggest
old shiny
secondhand Pierce Arrow in the house.
Ne' mind it might be too soft for his
pine hiney.

And he did, too. Went and came back blowing
A-ooga and jerking between gears like a blue
wheelbarrow.
We couldn't tell, for weeks, where he was going.
He had a look wider between the eyes than
the Pierce Arrow.

William D. Barney

Reprinted permission Prickly Pear Press,
The Kildeer Crying, 1977

1901

LENA THAYER; THE DOLLY MADISON OF THE MANSION

[*The title given to Lena Thayer by Texas newspapers in this period.*]

Lena awoke suddenly from her late afternoon nap. She sat up,
still tangled in wisps of fading dream, then rose to splash
water on her face and straighten her hair; looking in the glass
she saw clear ivory skin with a few lines and some sagging
at the oval chin line that told of middle age.

The soiree tonight would signal opening of the social season,
halfway through Joseph's second term as Governor of Texas.
She decided there would be time for one last look at the garden.

Lena's garden was only one of her many loves: she spoke French,
read poetry, painted portraits and was an accomplished pianist.

Peeking inside the library door on her way out, she smiled
to see Joseph busy at his desk with her pet cat, Beauty,
lying at his elbow; he loved that silly cat as much as she!

Beds of chrysanthemums held masses of October bloom. She broke
one white cluster and inhaled its sharp cold scent as she
sauntered along, remembering the garden's gone glories.

Circling the path by the rose garden, she stopped as a sudden
freshet of hot tears rolled down her cheeks and she dropped
to a nearby bench, groping for a handkerchief; she pressed
the scented linen to her streaming eyes and aching throat.

She mourned the martyred President, felled by an anarchist's
bullet only three weeks ago. Dear William and Ida McKinley!
Always so kind! She had sat on this same bench with Ida during
the presidential visit to Texas in May; how they had laughed
at shared memories of the long, good years in Washington!

After a few minutes, Lena's natural buoyancy returned.
She jumped up to pick the largest, reddest late-blooming rose,
then hurried back inside the mansion, thinking of her duties.

Ringing for her bath, she thought, I shall wear the pearl gray
velvet, with my garnet necklace and the red rose in my hair!

I shall play only light happy music tonight, Chopin and Strauss,
perhaps end with a Stephen Foster medley so everyone can sing.

One foot began tapping to the rhythm as she hummed,
then began to sing softly,

Camptown ladies sing this song,
Doo-dah! Doo-dah!

Helen Rilenge

1902

YEAR 1902 IN TEXAS HISTORY

In settling year nineteen-o-two,
With boundary wars ceased,
Young Texas land gobblers knew,
Down from the north and east.

Cheap right-of-ways attracted gold
For miles of new track laid;
And trains across expanses rolled
In pioneer parade.

Discrepancies arose with freight,
Demanding resolution;
And Jim Hogg's word carried weight
With the Railroad Commission.

Her first poll tax most whites embraced,
As Texas favored son;
And in gubernatorial race
Democrat Lanham won.

While ladies of the bar with charm
Stole hungry children's bread,
Poor Goliad, laid low with storm
And near two hundred dead.

While Presbyterian Austinites
Built their seminary,
Cattle ranchers fought for their rights
Fencing open prairie.

It was a year, like any year
With ups and downs galore—
Many a laugh and shed of tear,
But never a moment's bore.

William M. Murchison

1903

JOHN LANG SINCLAIR, CLASS POET

viewed by millions on network TV
how many fans giving Longhorn signs
have leaped to their feet
in stadium or stand
to resound his words throughout the land
inspired by Prather's paraphrase
of Robert E. Lee
locked by Lewis in room 305
of Brackenridge
he penned them on Bosch's
laundry paper in
nineteen three, like Rossini
who loved to eat
his meals brought up
and served to him
until he'd completed the overture
John Lang's friends forcing him
to finish the jest
in time for Varsity Minstrels in March
at the Hancock Opera House down on 6th
captive on his dormitory's
cold third floor
where before it rose so high
the water froze
yet flies were fewer there than home
the dairy farm on Joshua Creek
where hated milk drew
those lifelong enemies
though others saw and swear
his was the one unseen
meanwhile at the State
Track Meet each year
his "B" Hall's ascetic ways
paid off— star athlete
he biked to the Alamo
ran to Mount Bonnell and back
"a funny sort of a boy"
sat there composing at sunset
poems on the Texas norther
"comes sudden and soon
At the dead of night or the blaze of noon"
or during the smallpox epidemic
of please
anything but my vaccinated arm
"O the day was made for study
But the night for mirth and song"
on the choir trip by train
to Palestine
made goo-goo eyes at all the girls
a handsome guy who conversed
like "a cripple trying to walk"
his loyalty and zeal surpassed
any gift for carrying a tune
took up first the violin
but "swung such a squeaky bow"
was sent by his parents
out to practice
way far off
by the farm's dry well
near where a ranchhand
and his horse fell in
the hole found when
buzzards wheeled high overhead
from then on a spooky
place to all the kids
to Grace, President Prather's daughter
his poetry too gloomy
in tone too pessimistic
he however never doubted himself
it was just that he would put it off
as if he knew the saying
sometimes boomerangs
then left for Greenwich Village
as have so many since
till now our eyes are all on him
a judgment each must bear
the "livelong day"
have frittered our time away
talking the part
Bedichek never forgave
preferred him early
starved to death
than failing to give us
immortal verse
"He had the voice of Keats"
but who's to compete
with all it's meant
as stadiums fill with myriad mouths
rendering his *Eyes* countless as stars
in the
midnight skies
till Gabriel blows his horn
at Corregidor led by General Moore
a rival bunch of Aggies just imagine
sang his lines
"as a last shout of defiance"
imperial troops moving in for the kill
his blackface lyrics they never will
nor *Do not think you can escape them*
their "sleepless eyes" keep tireless vigil
expect us to with no truce no surrender

Dave Oliphant

SIX-SHOOTER JUNCTION

(to) Lon C. Hill: Your tenuous grasp slips. (1904?)
Your yellowing story brittles too fast —
let's flash it once more quick:

Ten miles long that road he graded —
by hand, by mule, by oil leaking tractor;
earning the admiration of mercenary mosquitoes
and frustrating small desert lizards
(blustering angrily away across the dry-cracked
clay-dust dirt). Quiet midwife.

Then posting aloft on lineman's jacks —
splintery purchase in dead spars
(scratching the soft sky with hard naked
skeletons of once proud pines), stringing stiff
wire telephone line 20 miles through prairie heat.
The contractions come quickly now.

Hammering brown dirt pounds the air flat and useless —
lungs become dense and hot (a dead yellow air
hissing sand and hatred at the trees, at the
dew-spotted web the dust spider spins, spraying
its intestines into silken geometry). The pain
is intense — it is a time of great doubt.

Patience. Patience. The time grows near.
Lon C. Hill shovels back the prairie's grasping
fingers and sweats again into the searing blue sky.
Mosquitoes blare their threatening descant.
Lizards watch.
The mother is dying.

A frightened groan. Dreams of bandidos and corn tortillas
skitter through her black fading eyes. Grapefruit
groves and old brown men squatting without words.
Watching Lon C. Hill's

hard, strong hands urge birth. Fitful revolution breeds hotly
behind the mesquite (only dead twitching:
the warm night air is sticky with blood-scent).

Six-Shooter Junction, your time is dry (wrinkled leather breasts
empty at last). Harlingen is born.

John B. Brisbin

ALIVE IN 1905

This year is history almost
So many happenings from coast to coast
Railroads building on every hand
Five this year across our land
Churches coming by the score
Baptist — Mennonites and more
Colleges and universities all about
A yearning for learning and things devout
Seven established this year alone
My how our facilities have grown
Hospitals and orphanages around our state
Our need for progress just can't wait
A library in Galveston for the blacks
First in the land from all our facts
A new office of Adjutant General
Large new strike in Humble's search for mineral
Daughters of Republic of Texas receive Alamo
As State Legislature makes it all so
New law for holding primary elections
State Tax Board for eternal collections
Counties organized named Terrell and Gaines
Surely not much else new remains
This next news I'm hesitant to give
Life's exciting in this time that we live
Would you believe everyone's going
To our theaters where movies are showing
In light of what's happening I can't wait till Spring
To see what nineteen hundred and six will bring!

N. W. Ogle

1906

HEADLINES BLARED
AND TOWNSPEOPLE STARED
"BELOVED SARA B' CAME TO TOWN."

Austin . . .
"a diamond in the rough"
"The Queen of the South" struggled to shake the western image
Her yellow clay streets were riddled with rutted wagon ridges
muddy water — filled holes after thirst drenching skies

Blacks and whites, one walking on wooden plank walkways
the other, "steps down" to let "them whites" pass by!

Hardware stores and lumberyards
Chinese laundries and boardinghouses
horse drawn wagons
took new immigrants to limestone hotels,
thrifty farmers from the midwest
high class people with money to invest.

On a hot summer day, a parade of passing troops
a clatter of horse hoofs and clanking sabers
the cavalry marching amid the flag lined streets.
After the long march from San Antonio
they encamped by Barton Springs . . . destination . . .
Camp Mabry. Old soldiers remember.

During the pecan harvest, a lone Lobo wolf roamed the town
captured . . . tied and left to die. He escaped
and slinked to hide in Hyde Park, only to be captured again.

In the shade of the dome of the great granite capitol
on land where once Indians roamed and mesquite bushes grew
a giant tent opera house appeared.
Headlines blared and townspeople stared
on stage the "Divine Sarah Bernhardt" . . .
Ah, *Camille!*
Culture had come to Austin.

The city was journeying into the future,
politician and entrepreneur, citizen and immigrant
Congress Avenue with paving, new bridges,
roller skating, summer theater, automobiles and ordinance:
any guilty will be arrested.
Austin would not be held back,
she wore her "Violet crown" but she had not reached her zenith . . .

Pat Wissler

1907

REMINISCENCE

Old folk reminiscing "how it used to be"
Can give valuable facts of our city's history.
They were remembering the streetcar line
Though dim the present — past memory is fine.
Here we record bits of information
We were able to capture from their conversation:

> "In 1907, the Nobles brothers M. C. and H. A.
> Organized the Amarillo Street Railway
> With Banker Paul and J. W. Crudgington
> They drove gold spike — the project begun.
> It was Mayor Miller swinging hammer first
> With civic pride — our city was aburst.
> Looking down Polk — that dirt street was alive
> With wagons, horses, Model Ts — counted five.
> Who was that went into Red Front Saloon?
> 'Wet' or 'Dry' election's being held soon.
> That was the year Potter County voted 'Dry'
> Ha! thought some those ol' boys 'ld die.
> Building was booming — what was new?
> Two-story Chanslor Building, Grand Opera House too
> and the Morrow–Thomas Hardward
> Had harness, bridles, wagons, Queensware
> Carriages, windmills and supplies
> Such a selection laid out 'fore our eyes."

They rode seven miles on that streetcar track.
It took them crosstown and brought them back.
They settled and rocked, continued to tell
How Amarillo grew — they knew it so well.

Juanita Roberts

1908

THE MISSION

1908, and the Battle of the Alamo raged on. No bloodied
Crocketts or Jim Bowies guard the cradle this time. Only
Adina De Zavala, five feet tall and tiny-boned will stand
and hold the fort. No troops of Santa Anna's come attacking,
but all around the mission the hungry eyes of hotel plans
and knickknack shops draw closer.

February 10th, she locks herself inside the walls of independence
and will not leave despite the sheriff. And so he sees
that no one enters, that no one gives her any food.
He does allow her water, though, provided it is poured
through the peephole of the door. Stooping, Adina catches the water
in her mouth, the flavor of the battle swirling
across her tongue. Standing, she sees the history of Texas
in the walls, feels the coolness in her mouth, then swallows
thirstily of both.

Eleventh of February and the title to the property is transferred
to the state. Developers defeated, Adina walks outside and stares.
No blood is on the ground, yet a battle has been fought, and blood
within the walls is flowing — the Alamo will live,
Adina's mission is complete.

José Luis Parra

1909

ELISABET NEY MUSEUM

Formosa

Familiar as those summer afternoons
I spent padding along the creekbanks,
Watching the clouds upon clouds pouring
Over the turrets and towers crowning
Your home, my castle.

Unfolding my childhood dreams
And wild imaginings while I played
In the dank, dim rooms, vacant shuttles
Weaving the wind, whistling through
The stones, I climbed the circular stairs,
Leaning far out the deep windows, hoping

To catch a ghostly glimpse of your Grecian
Robes, stirring up dust, flying along in
A chariot, or appearing behind the cupboard
Door, one hand on the knob.

You left only the silence of huge voices
Calling to one another across time —
Garibaldi, Bismarck, Ludwig, all giants,
Carved in a final whiteness, the lost
Energies frozen, becoming a kind of peace,

At last, as they congregate in the brilliant
Light, cool, white, Carrara marble —
Blind angels and pillars of salt,
Still touch my heart.

Mary Esther Frederick

LETTER FROM TEXAS

I dreamed I found some cloth you sent me years ago
You remember yards of fabric, how we loved to sew in our young days

Enough for two gowns, no, more — but in the dream I added a yard
of stuff, seems to me muslin, some sort of sprigged flower grows here,
and that I paid too much, terribly dear

I'll never forget the care I took to make a dress I could unhook
to bare the breast, this was when the baby was new
and needing my milk on the hour

You know I'm not one to save each little thing
but I thought I must have a button somewhere,
a scrap of that cloth I could hold onto

The dress was so clear in the dream
I woke to search my sewing kit, desperate for a button
Seeing it, pink, cream, mother of pearl, the slight rise,
the curve of the edge of it wouldn't slip through

My fingers remembered as I slept the button shank and the thread
they used to anchor it down
How I pricked myself, bled a tiny spot on the new gown
Odd to picture it now, with button and dress nowhere to be found
Just a bit of thread, a scrap of lace

But the thing which disturbs me more than the dream, or even
that the baby is grown with children,
and buttons, scraps, patches crying out to be sewn

Is that I remember this button and cloth far better than our mother's face
Oh, probably I gave the dress away
Or was it misplaced in a move farther west?

And now, perhaps I shall sleep

Give the folk of Fermanagh, in Ireland, all of my best
for the chance of my finding either button or dress is the same
as that I shall leave this state to greet them again,
or probably less

Patricia Reinhardt Monaco

1911

MAY 21, 1911

  The Pecos *Daily Times* said
fire made man the ruler of the world
  peace in Mexico tonight
  word has come from Juarez
  enemies scribbling their names
  in the glare of auto lights
  the border sighs; the troops will leave the coast
  and the *Times* said
man must have fuel to have fire
  nine hundred mothers wives sisters of Austin
  begged the governor to forsake the Demon
  Carry Nation was dying in Kansas
  a Henderson missionary
  seeking converts in Africa
  found malaria instead
and the fuel is here
  the salutatorian of the class of 1911 said
  we are Hannibal crossing the Alps
  a river of oil burst from Electra
  Rinche burst through border children's nightmares
those with fuel will rule
  the salutatorian said
  we are on the Acropolis of Italy
  yonder lies Rome
  Pecos has five good hotels and needs more
  and the *Times* said
we are closing out our chickens
this is your very last chance

Roland E. Sodowsky

THE ALCOHOL QUESTION

Whether to drink or not to drink: that was
The fiery issue in Texas in 1912.
Did individuals have a sacred right
Or even a secular right to ruin lives?
To live in a state of liberty allowed
Or patriotically required a man
To be free to do almost anything he wanted.
But did murders and rapes — bad things — increase because
Of gin? rum? whiskey? — even beer and wine?
Hard question. Commissions studied it. Why not
Allow a man, after a hard day's work,
To seek stimulus, followed by anesthesia.
Many were happy drunks. But the blind rage
In some between first shot and sodden sleep
Was bothersome: the deaths; the broken homes . . .
Perhaps an amendment to the Constitution?
Texans continued to think, and drink. The end
Of Governor O. B. Colquitt's four-year term
Saw alcohol cussed, discussed, and swallowed down,
And the question of prohibition unresolved.

Thomas Whitbread

LONESOME TEXAS

He lay down his hoe, left his cornfield on the side
of Hammer Mountain. Ira Hammer came to Texas
on the Soash Emigrant train. He built a house,
and he built a school before he sent for Kate
and the children. Kate grew silent when she saw
the prairie free from rivers and trees — free
from a swinging bridge. Ira built her a two-story
house. Not like she left in West Virginia — not ten
rooms but two. Two stories high, one atop the other.
Kate doffed her white linen dress and lace gloves,
and removed her black plumed hat to pick up cowchips.
She climbed the windmill to cut meat from a side of beef
hanging there. Lonesome Texas, she named the land.
"An abstract title that promised to pass muster with
a square deal all around." And they had bought the farm.

The wind in West Texas could teach the breeze
in Franklin, W.V., how to do sixty by 8 A.M.
The wind that picked up pieces of dirt that settled
on the white clothes until they were the color
of Mama's gravy. Even the white leghorn hens were
a coal miner's gray. In letters home, she boasted
about the milo maize making forty-five bushels
and kafircorn that made forty. Ira wrote
in his diary, "Next year. Next year, when we
have money. Next year when everything is good."
Two children later (he had stopped counting
how many *next years* had passed) they sold a farm.
Sold part of the land and rented out the rest.
Sold the car, and boarded the train in Plainview.
Kate in her plumed hat, and he in his best gray suit,
with moustache trimmed went back to tell the folks
about their home in the West. They were elegant
in their good taste. Six months later, back
in Texas in time to start over. To get ready
for next year, picking up cowchips, and watching
wind push tumbleweeds that would never arrive
in West Virginia: Even the wind refused
to blow in that direction.

Bettye Givens

1914

CHRISTMAS

Standing on the porch,
Her back to the fading fires of sunset,
She breathes in senses of the waning day:
Spicy fragrance of pumpkin, cookies,
Excited shrill of children,
Flickers like firebugs as streetlamps are lit,
Coughing cars backfire snapping at barking dogs,
Faint whinny of the iceman's impatient horse,
Heavy tang of sea in the chilly air.
Pulling her woolen shawl closer,
She shivers to ward off the icy sadness.

Euphoric in the morning, she watched
Steamer creak slowly into the dock —
Tired old trader ready for its bed.
He came from the ship to her,
Holding her fiercely, mutely,
Only the gauntness in his eyes betraying
Pain, fear, destruction of the war in Europe.
They walked down tree lined avenues,
Past the ice cream wagon and its gentle mare,
Past the cold marble monument to war,
Past children playing stickball in the street.

Now in the growing darkness, he comes to her,
His arms seeking comfort in her closeness.
Voices of carolers float softly through the dusk,
Music swells through diamond studded sky,
Words wash over him, soothing and familiar.
Oh, come all ye faithful, joyful . . .
Smiling, they turn toward the glow of the house,
Walk into the warmth of Christmas, of home.

Patty O'Briant Anderson

1915: *THE TRANSITION*
FAREWELL TO *A WAY OF LIFE*

Pillowed on clouds and wings of air, the gods had fallen asleep somewhere.
With never a warning to mark the day, when forever, the old life slipped away.

Such a happy, uncomplicated, peaceful world. An extraordinary time, those years *before*
1915. America at its best. Generations who believed, acted, lived with confidence in
Their ability to change the world, subdue the enemy, and rebuild the ruins. Expected
To change things, *and they did.* Glimpses back are kaleidoscopic: A high, wide and
Handsome era. Large flamboyant houses, grand balls — for the richer. For the poor:
Cotton fields, or crowded cities and $3.50 a week. Little boys rolled hoops with a stick
Along ditches where family cows were staked. Girls fresh from curling irons
Hopscotched secure and quiet streets. Women chatted over fences, clothes billowed on
Clotheslines. Where the pump had been in the kitchen was *plumbing*; where kerosene
Lamps and gaslights once glowed was *electricity.* There was china, crystal, solid
Mahogany and walnut furniture. All the outward trappings of families whose solidity
Has all but vanished. Picnics with biscuits and fried chicken and yellowjackets on
The watermelon. Glorious *un*safe Fourths of July, crowds gathered to hear the orators,
The Flag! and memories of ancestors . . . while electric streetcars jingled. The family
Buggy, stable, horses, dogs, and kittens nestled in strawy barns like Easter eggs
Hidden in the grass. By 1910, Texas had the whole U.S. Air Corps: one plane and
One pilot who taught himself to fly. The gods woke up then!

"Now what is that I hear below? Isn't that where the Alamo . . ."
"Yes," answered thoughtful War God Mars, (contemplating future wars),
"Man has learned to fly."

And man had learned to drive . . . The automobile had chugged into towns with
Drama. Distances — and people — could be closer, now. And what a People! They
Reformed the wicked, fed the hungry, paraded with the Suffragettes. They remarked
It was a time of triumph: Airplanes, cars, ships . . . They *did* get taxes in 1913,
Too bad eggs were ten cents to a quarter a dozen and steak was thirty cents a pound,
But — they'd cope.

Then, somnolent gods and live oak trees, woke from their tranquillities,
Even the bustle of cities had grown, quiet as grass, and still as stone . . .

We were a nation *on the verge of war.* The pilot who'd flown old Number One built the
First airdrome — in Texas. At our late entry into battle, the men would march off to
Win the war to end all wars singing . . . like actors offstage. In 1915, women whispered
In the night, *I'm afraid it will be all different . . . somehow.* And it was. The old life was
Slipping away, and the wise knew it almost at once. Simple problems vanished.
So did simple solutions. The lights didn't exactly go out, nor the music stop,
But that wonderful time would never return again.

Shirley Denise Ratisseau

1916

THE POWER

Go down, Moses,
harpoon the spider who
submarines truth;
like the Ancient Mariner, I make
my albatross my standard;
I wear it, bleeding, thumping warm death
against my broken breast,
but I will not give my hand

Go down, Moses,
with your stone tablets
chisel one more thou shalt not;
generations born of the soil, all
those born to be protected
from spinners of grief — they
know me as brother;
I am their Farmer Jim.
Our glasses raise, we toast
each other; the fruit of Lucifer
will not cross our lips

And, the spider sits,
watching my triumph,
carefully building his
tangled web

Go down, Moses,
send for Minerva,
my integrity is turned inside out,
the power is wrenched from me;
the demon spider spits out
regents, all shouting obscenities;
"impeach — impeach — impeach — "
angry echoes, thunder to fill galleries,
thunder like a range stampede
snorting fire, their long horns impale me —

My bush is burning,
I go down, Moses,
but I will not give my hand

J. G. Butts

TAKEOFF INTO WAR

Before the runway ends, the small plane lifts
into the air, wavers, circles the field gaining
altitude, flies true. On his third solo flight,
the student pilot comes down on his wheels,
bounces onto the nose, and breaks the propeller.
That record is in my father's pilot book.
Years later, he'll tell me the propeller
replica on his desk was made from

the grained red wood of the prop he broke.
He trained at Kelly, near San Antonio,
the largest flying field of the Great War.
The century was as young as those who enlisted
"to end all wars." Dad's voice quickens
and rises when he describes the open
land and Texas heat, how they drilled in
pursuit, bombing, map making, aerobatics . . .

In an army photo, my father stands next
to his Curtiss JN4D biplane, one hand
on a strut, the wind thrumming the craft
till it quivers, ready to go. His new
silver wings shine above his breast pocket.
Beneath the helmet his eyes, the color
of twilight sky, range past me.
His white scarf snaps and rolls.

Jean H. Marvin

THE YEAR OF THE WOMEN

With only seventeen days
Remaining in that July.
Suffragettes prepared the women of Texas.
They sent them half a million
Copies of unofficial ballots.
Singly and by twos and threes
The women came from far and wide
To qualify as electors, made eligible
This year: freed, enfranchised
To vote in all the primaries,
Nominate in district conventions.

The women learned to scrutinize
The candidates. They knew the issues.

Following their chief leader,
Minnie Fisher Cunningham,
"Snatching from the griddle" the hot
Political pancake,
In this one party state,
Equality with men,
Three hundred eighty six thousand
Women registered as citizens to vote.

At the polls they showed a force
Unheard of and unknown before this date.

Lorene Pouncey

1919

1919 ELBOWED IN

With all their medals,
With all their tears
The war times dwarfed
The following years,

But into brash Texas
1919 elbowed in —
He was not a brother;
He was not a twin.

The winds of change
Were buffeting all,
And business boomed
To Capital's call.

Early in the year
A hurricane
Gave Corpus Christi
Great loss and pain,

And Hockaday,
One woman's dream,
Became a girls' school,
The crème de la crème.

Bob-haired "gals" smoked and drank
And drove fast cars,
And their fight to vote
Was a dozen wars.

They won their battle
To force the truth
In the working place
And the voting booth,

And dancing in
A partner's arms
A la the Castles
Had its many charms.

Texas times were changing
With a sigh and a dimple,
And life would never
Again be simple.

Robby K. Mitchell

1920

A LA 1920s

Your visage then, Tejas,
was fraught with bigness,
the largest star in the 48,
your legislature passed
the nineteenth, stating
women could now vote, yet
they still had much struggle
facing them as did countless
tens of thousands streaming
through your cotton rows;

a short lived depression,
WW I vets returned,
voters eliminated limits
on school tax rates,
your cities entered junior college
fields, El Paso fielded its first j.c.,

and on that January 16th, the holy 18th
ran amuck — against unholy demon rum —
so that contrabandistas would proliferate
in song and deed, bootleg-whiskeying
your border city gambling dens;

yes, General Pershing visited you
with Villa's footprints engraved
rustily upon his brow;
Baytown birthed the 2nd largest refinery,
while Dallas, Houston, and San Antonio
would house o'er a 100,000 souls,
Omar Locklear would die a-filming, never
to walk from plane-to-plane again!

Concrete linked San Benito to Harlingen,
at Kelly Field someone rip-corded his parachute,
oh, yes, my natal land,
you did produce some gold
    five fine ounces worth a hunnerd-bucks,
El Paso doubled its population, and
in the main, you became
a larger Tejas, brimming with
    love, discontent, and a future
geared to someday struggle
to in-corporate your children . . .

Ricardo Sánchez

AMARILLO
FROM RAGTOWN TO BOOMTOWN

Itches for riches which had infected landowners
since before the turn of the century
was consumated by millions, beginning in the year 1921,
when the first oil well spewed liquid gold
into the fresh, pure air of the Texas Panhandle.
Suddenly, the earth was erupting a rash of gushers and gas wells
in a field of derricks, thick as the prairie dog mounds.
Agriculture sank to second place, in the economy.

The original settlement was pioneered by hunters of the bison
with only a few crude dwellings, built of buffalo hides.
Migrating farmers, discovering the fertility of the soil
began growing crops and grazing cattle.
Cowboys, in boots, saddles, and violent weather,
tended their herds and fought cattle rustlers.
Wives cooked out-of-doors and cleared away tumbleweeds, for gardens.
Saturday nights, everyone put away cares to hop bars
and square dance to the music of fiddles and guitars.

In 1887, the town was incorporated and christened, *Ragtown.*
It was later renamed, *Amarillo,* a Spanish word meaning yellow.
A Mexican herdsman had previously given the name
to nearby Amarillo Lake — for its yellow banks.

The scent of *Black Gold,* spread by geologists
attracted capitalists and brought about the strike of '21.
Hordes of people thronged to the area, like ants to honey pots.
Under the influence of *Lucre and Liquor, the Petro twins,*
people changed overnight, assuming a devil-may-care attitude to life.
at a time when *Flappers* and *Jellybeans* were doing the Charleston
into the wee hours, all across the nation.
Flappers flaunting sexuality in short skirts and rolled hose
bobbed their hair and wore makeup for the first time in history.
Jellybeans, wearing bell-bottom trousers, slicked their hair
and parked *Tin Lizzies* on country roads, to snuggle with sweethearts.

Time passed, wild capers died out, and Amarillo began to groom itself
for rapid developments in education, industry, and the arts.

If this proud metropolis is, now, on a roll,
credit should go to the year 1921, for first oiling its wheels.

Ruby Hughes Bussey

1922

INCIDENT AT BATTLE CREEK

[*The Klan in politics*]

All robed and hooded they came on horseback to
semicircle our front gate and hello the house.
Anachronistic as dinosaurs, they had risen again
from the putrid morass of ignorance, hate and
prejudice like the miasma over rotting carcasses.
They came to get Pa; not to tar and feather, not to
whip, but to enlist his support in their nefarious
deeds.
"You know why we've come. We want you to help us rid
this community of niggers, mesicans, jews and
idolatrous catholics."
Then we recognized the voice — our preacher!
"No," Pa said. "These folks are gentle people and
good neighbors. And you, Ben, if you want to
disguise yourself with sheet and pillowcase,
better leave that swaybacked gray at home. Homer
should not ride that saddle mule."
On and on he went, identifying each in spite of robe
and hood. One rider pulled away, then another
vanished in the darkness until only the leader remained.
"Go on home, Preacher. You ain't a bad man, just
ignorant. Go on home."
He went.
The next night a fiery cross burned before our gate.

Bevington Reed

1923

HEMPSTEAD, 1923

[*For my Grandparents*]

The main street flanked by shabby storefronts, dust
Motes slowly floating in the heat, the hours
Expand to memory. The farmers drive
To town each Saturday. Their faces scan
The sky before they talk about their maize
And cotton, watermelons cracking in
The sun, the campaign of Ma Ferguson.
The cotton gins are running now. Their fierce
Teeth grind out perfect bales from August to
October, giant seeds enclosed in steel,
While linseed oil drips through the years. Across
The street the house still stands, the picket fence
Implied, the swing and pomegranate trees
Almost restored. The silent rooms, the steep
White gables hidden in the trees suggest
The possibility of sound: a sharp
Swift clattering of feet along the stairs,
A spate of scales extracted from the old
Belligerent piano after school,
The lazy whine of ceiling fans, the blades
Describing sleepy circles on the walls.
Above all else, the yearly music of
The tree, a Brazos cedar twelve feet tall,
Unwilling to be dragged along the porch
And crowded through the door, the sullen swish
Of sodden, rainsoaked branches in the hall,
The scent of dark green needles covering
The floor. Those sounds continue somewhere, in
Some other rooms and isolated thoughts.
Around the graves there's just the distant barking
Of a dog, the crawling of two ants
Across the stone, the sprouting of a black
Eyed susan in the soft red clay, their small
Acts muffled in the fog that rolls in off
The Gulf. Remote events enclosed by time,
They still suggest the possibility of sound.

Carol Coffee Reposa

1924

TEXAS TUNES

[David Wendell Guion, 1892–1981]

It has been said of David Wendell Guion that
He set our history to music for the world
To hear, preserving it for all posterity.
He had a poet's perception to appreciate
The music at his own back door, the ranch out west.
Old Negro spirituals his Mammy Nepie sang
As lullabies, the cowboy ballads, fiddle tunes —
All these Guion arranged for the piano.
Sometimes his music would not keep or let him sleep.
He studied in Vienna, taught for many years,
performed on radio, at Madison Square Garden,
At Carnegie Hall and Radio City Music Hall.
In 1924, at Roxy Theater
He starred in *Prairie Echoes*, his own cowboy hit,
The first old western musical on New York stage.
Home on the Range was President Roosevelt's favorite song;
He liked *The Yellow Rose of Texas* too. New York
Acclaimed Guion the modern Stephen Foster, and
Red China's band hailed Nixon with *Home on the Range*.
Guion recordings were a cultural exchange
With Russia to promote goodwill. His manuscripts
Were given to The University of Texas.
The Houston Symphony premiered his *Texas Suite,*
And Toscanini first performed his *Turkey in*
The Straw. Caruso, Crosby, church choirs, and the Met
All sang Guion's toe-tapping, hand-clapping, heartwarming tunes.
His prayer in nights of fears that God keep open his heart
And mind, his eyes and ears should be our prayer to share
Worldwide, promoting brotherhood through history,
Inspiring other hearts to hum with harmony.

Marjorie Ledbetter Yelton

1925

THE FLAME, THE CROSS, THE SIN, THE VEIL

His Rosa sits within the dark confessing.
She comes each week, a weeping ragged bundle,
her hands and heart a knot of guilt and fear.
She doesn't know her sin but yet her husband's
dead. She fears the cross more than she should.
Where is the power, where is the golden glory?
Where is the strength, the fury and the flame?
Where is the law that rules above all others?
She doesn't ask all that. Her Manuel's dead —
that's all she has to say. She knows. I know.
The Klan has waned, has fallen out of favor,
but last year in the midst of the election
cowled figures rode the countryside at night.
Not here, I thought, please let them not ride here.
Then came the night I heard the hooves outside.
Did he commit a crime? It didn't matter.
They chained him to a tree, beat him, whipped him,
turned loose their dogs and finally cut his throat.
And all for what? Who knows? The governor,
they say, has stopped the Klan. I guess it's true.
And yet, no one's confessed the murder and
no one's been brought to trial. And no one yet
has even been arrested. Why? She knows.
His blood, dried on the grass, was flecked with dew.
I saw.
            Hail Marys won't help. What good are they
when God himself won't try? I tell her what
I can, to go in peace. (She has no sin.)

I can't tell when she leaves. I have no sign.

Things go unmarked. Men live and die. No one
will mark the tree. No one will tend his grave.

The unknown sin cannot be cleansed.

                                        My God!
That night, of all the nights, you made me ride . . .

Alan Birkelbach

THE SPIRIT OF 1926

A young generation was testing its wings
in the "roaring twenties,"
and 1926 was in the middle of it all.
Young women disdained the styles of bygone days.
It was the "flapper" age.
They wore long waisted
short skirted dresses
bobbed their hair
danced the Charleston
smoked cigarettes
wore tight bathing suits.

The issue of prohibition was with us.
To drink or not to drink
was a question facing youth.
Young men wore silk shirts
snazzy two-toned spats
danced the Charleston
played the ukelele
smoked Lucky Strikes
drove Model Ts.

"Honest Dan" Moody was our governor —
young, handsome and brilliant.
He was the youngest governor of Texas
married Mildred Paxton of Abilene
went on "honeymoon campaign"
Hardin–Simmon's Cowboy Band
played at his inauguration
won the governorship twice
noted for improving our highways.

Texas enjoyed a year of
prosperity and growth
in 1926.

Garnet Quiett

POEM TO MA FERGUSON

I've been sleeping out, Miriam, sleeping out on county land, working at getting the bucks together to rent a place, and so public places like our state capitol are good for hanging out, passing time like all the old coots in Stetsons outside on park benches, crackerbarrel wisdom even here in the 1980s —

So now I sit on a wooden chair in capitol rotunda, tourists all around me craning their necks up — up into blue dome — here I sit, staring at your pleasant face, Ma Ferguson, first oil portrait to the right of south entrance. Although your dress leaves shoulders bare, to be half covered by a shawl, the artist hasn't painted you Hollywood pretty. The chin is solid, marked with a cleft; your eyes are set in a serious thinking frown; your cheeks, though rouged, are firm. Miriam. Ma Ferguson — Texas's first woman governor — two terms yet. Two more paintings down and there you are again, older now, plumper, flecks of gray in your hair, grandmotherly, no shoulders bare.

Ma, you caught a lot of flak, a lot of anti-feminist flak during both your terms of office; some just didn't like it when you said "many women will be invited to take an active part in this administration." First woman governor of Texas from a family with flash and flamboyance — you passed a law that made it a crime to wear the Klan's white hood in public place. Your daughter says you were tough minded — tough enough not to fear advice from your husband Governor Jim. A woman — you know how they say — has got to be twice as good as a man.

Ma Ferguson, Texas's first woman governor . . . for a man like me, sleeping out in my car in a camp like the Hoovervilles of the Depression, you mean something. A symbol. Right or wrong, you and your husband gave the impression at least that you cared for the little man. I remember you saved a young Chicano from the electric chair because it was his first offense. You symbolized something yes here in Texas, something we need to remember here in the greedy 1980s when a B-movie actor strides this land playing Hollywood rhinestone cowboy — symbolized — shall I call it maternal? — a love for our sisters and brothers, progressive populism.

Chuck Taylor

1928

BEFORE AND AFTER

it was just before
the dive
into the
desperation
of the Depression

it was just after
the burials of
the first
World
War

it was the year
Dan Moody won
reelection

the year Kate Oliver
was birthed
in Mexia

it was the final
twirl of the Roaring Twenties
tornadoing across the bluebonneted hills

of Texas

Sheryl L. Nelms

THE BETSY ROSS OF TEXAS

[From an old newspaper clipping, Houston, January 9th 1929. Regina Stopple's husband, C. W. Stopple, invented the percussion caps used by Confederate soldiers.]

The casual motorists
Who waited impatiently
For the brief procession to pass,
Did not know that one of the South's unsung heroines
Was on her way to her last resting place.

They called her Regina, the Betsy Ross of the South.
I remember her as slight,
Her gray hair pulled tightly back above her brow.
Yet even then, as a child, I saw in those dark eyes,
A tenderness almost too large
For one lone heart to hold.

She never spoke of those bad times
So many Autumns ago,
When agony was more than just a word
Spelled out between the North and South.
Each season knows its own despair:
Enough that she had worked and wept and waited —
She had no need to speak.

And yet there was that secret smile.
We watched not knowing
How great or small a thing she bore.

Was she thinking of those women, so long ago,
Who met each weekday at the old Cathedral
On Caroline street?
Met to cut and rip the already tattered cloth,
To make whole uniforms from remnants —
Patching woefully worn rags of gray?
Working and praying for their soldiers?

Was she feeling with those frail fingers, even then,
The coat she once had fashioned for the great Dick Dowling,
Hero of the South?

We do not know.
All we have now is this yellowed newspaper clipping
And a faded photograph, to tell the story
Of one who lived and loved
And never dreamed of glory.

Libby Stopple

1930

TEXAS, OUR TEXAS

[*State song, initiated by Governor Pat Neff, approved by the Legislature 1930; lyrics by Gladys Wright and W. J. Marsh, music by Marsh.*]

Texas for years needed
  a song,
A dramatic tribute but
  not too long;
An official song for
  Texans alone,
One true to their heritage
  and maybe prone
To brag a little about
  their "great:"
The heroes of freedom and
  Alamo fate.

Marsh and Wright entered
  competition
Open to all and on its
  completion
Emerged with a song, and
  Texans were proud
To tell it as it was, and
  they "allowed"
It showed their spirit in
  true Texas manner
With added love for Lone
  Star Banner.

Texans stood tall as their
  music rang out;
They responded clearly with
  a hearty shout:
"Texas, our Texas! All hail
  the mighty state."
"We love and honor thee, O
  greatest of the great!"

Lillian Davis Terrill

V
Hard Times
1930–1939

Hard times were no novelty to Texas farmers because they had been suffering from low cotton prices and lack of profit before the stock market crash. They blamed this situation on hard money policies and tariffs, both beyond their control. Nature was against the farmer and rancher. Drouth stinted crops, and brought choking dust and there were plagues of grasshoppers. Winter cold killed cattle, even milch cows. Disheartened, some headed for California and abandoned their farms. The Great Depression further aggravated their problems, and resulted in some farmers being sold out for mortgage or tax delinquency, but the majority stayed on farms and ranches to eke out a precarious existence.

City dwellers faced unemployment for there was little work of any kind to be had, unemployment was rife. Despite various programs initiated by the government to bring relief, there was little overall improvement until the late 1930s. Texans were faced with the dilemma of accepting and of participating in programs sponsored by the government that ran counter to their basic distaste for such intervention.

Conditions did not change very much until the war in Europe increased the demand for Texas products: cotton, synthetic rubber and various industrial chemicals. When Texas became a gigantic training base for the Army and Navy, there was the construction of new bases and the enlargement of existing bases to create work.

The people of Texas were totally committed to the support of the war effort.

THE BALLAD OF BONNIE AND CLYDE

[*Written to the tune of "Frankie and Johnny" an irregular ballad.*]

Bonnie Parker was a slip of a waitress
Weighing less than ninety-nine pounds,
When Clyde Barrow saw her slinging hash
In a diner at the edge of town.
He got on her trail, like an old bloodhound . . .
Like an old bloodhound.

Clyde got thrown in the slammer
His sentence was five years long.
"I'm going to spring my man," Bonnie said
"But I gotta be strong . . ."
Smiling through her tears, "I just gotta be strong."

Bonnie and Clyde became robbers
Had themselves barrels of fun
Shooting all over the countryside
With their stolen .38 gun.
Oh, they were lovers, but they had to run . . .
They had to run.

Brother Buck and Blanche joined the gang
Leaving a long bloody trail
Throughout Texas, Oklahoma, Louisiana
Spreading their Barrow hell . . .
Spreading their Barrow hell.

Bonnie was cute and desiring
She soon got tired of the pace
Of dodging through brambles and hamlets
With the lawmen in hot chase.
Oh, they were lovers, but they ran the race
. . . they ran the race.

I'm going to end this saga
With words of Bonnie, herself:
"Someday we'll go down together
They'll bury us side by side.
To a few it'll be grief—
To the law, a relief
But it'll be death for Bonnie and Clyde."

Esther Lee Thompson

UNCLE HEDLEY* AND HARD TIMES

[**Name changed to protect the guilty.*]

The prairie was level as a threshing floor.
Early surveyors, with Jacob's staff and chain,
Had laid in squares and sections all the plain
For town and farmsite. Where buffalo once wore

Their paths to anciently discovered hollows,
Uncle Hedley's farm by lot was set.
Outside his gate, whenever the season was wet,
The soil, all talcum-fine in the animals' wallow,

Was mud. So Uncle Hedley cussed the rain
And towed out Studebaker and Model T,
Drawn by his patient mules from the oozy sea.
The Great Depression struck like a hurricane.

Then he shot rabbits with his twenty-two,
Cooking them with spuds from his garden plot.
One day he could find not a single one for his pot,
So scooped up rabbit tracks from the snow, to stew

With carrots and onions from their summer's canning.
Uncle Hedley abandoned his country pride
And charged a dollar for every car he pried
From the wallow. Neighbors hinted that his planning

Went further: Unkind grapevine rumors said
That midnight found him dumping barrels of water
Into the fine-grained soil, to insure each auto
Would bog to its hubcaps. Thus was his family fed

On rabbits tracked through crisp, unmelted snow
And cars he pulled from the wallow of the buffalo.

Bessie May Hill

1932

A POTPOURRI OF MEMORIES

Although a new year had arrived on the scene,
The Depression lingered on like a relative
reluctant to leave.
On the radio, Rudy Vallee (megaphone in hand)
Still crooned in his own inimitable way —
While that same old Philco brought us the humorous
Lum and Abner show at the close of day.
Hobos arrived at our back door so often they were
no longer "unexpected guests."
After handing them a filled plate, ". . . plain fare
but nourishing," Mom would say,
(She could never bear to turn one away.)
Miriam Ferguson, one half of the "Jim and Ma"
controversial gubernatorial team —
Was making new headlines on the Texas political scene,
(Ma had decided to run for governor again, it seemed)
Meanwhile FDR's New Deal was really making waves,
"It's a 'raw deal,' " was what the opposition raved.
Hemlines were a barometer of the times, it was said,
Short skirts like in the early twenties meant good times,
Mid-calf, as in the thirties signaled hard times ahead!
As a teenager I hated to see the flapper styles fade.
But that year Empress Eugenie hats became the latest craze.
Only recently had our movie house been wired for sound,
And I was eagerly awaiting *The Jazz Singer* to come to our town.
(Then too, a new boy moved in two doors down.)
We were caught in the middle of what had been —
and . . . what was to come.
A potpourri of events that is true,
For that was the great year of 1932!

Beatrice M. Land

THE NEW DEAL

In the thirty-three years since the turn
with this century's desire, burning to learn,
the hustle, and bustle slow to the market's tune,
while busting many a dream-filled balloon.

Hoover thought the nation more sturdy
as lack of trade brought luck down and dirty.
Between investors, court jesters, and rule testers,
we saw more poor and distraught from bad guessers.

FDR was made a star with his New Deal,
and got the country's boat working for an even keel.
The panic caused the great negative flow
to wreak the worst havoc history came to know.

Depressed and regressed Texans felt the pain
of greed and mistrust falling like unrelented rain,
and lines in many faces grew, as shuffled paces and
holes in shoes
with lines for bread proving good food for only a few.

Congress knew Agriculture Adjustments were sorely due,
and industries helped the U.S.A. to recover anew.
Improving labor and money control were at the root.
Propelled by the feeling of what had to be one, giving a hoot,
leaders predicted it wouldn't be a turkey shoot.

The President upped attitudes with fireside chats,
telling fear was the only fear, and to combine in Depression
combat.

America joined together to beat the odds,
and changed to positive the continuing nods.
Roosevelt asserted his electric mind
to affect social uncertainty and dissension for all time.

Terry Cole

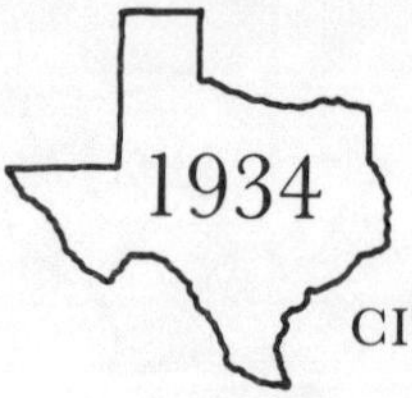

CIVILIAN CONSERVATION CORPS, FORT DAVIS, TEXAS

[*To the Men of C.C.C. Companies 879 and 881 — especially Ernesto Rivera and Dr. Alfred Pfitsch, Jr.*]

[Roosevelt, 1933]

Advisors that night had talked a great deal
then left him alone on his pillows of smoke.
Whether within or without were alms best to heal,
the argument turned on the forms of one's hope.
Like a crippled king in his crippled sleep
he called them back to hold their holder
at jaunty angles, new chanticleer of Walden;
but the country was broke and heading for broken,
the men with "lives of quiet desperation . . ."

The painted old man on the horse on the hill
invaded the dream with a circling red arm:
"*The Earth Understands*!"

And so the Corps was commissioned.

[Builders, 1934]

From Alpine to Marfa down Limpia Canyon to chisel the rock,
ring the skyline with the raw roads, bake brown adobe,
machete tall reeds from the Rio Grande,
lay alligator juniper into patterns of Indian Lodge.

[Visitors, 1984]

Condensation channels down super-cooled aluminum
into saffron sunsets on hand-cut cedar,
circle stains of affluent thirst.

The furniture in this room was made by the C.C.C.
Help us preserve it. Please use the coasters.

"Desk wiggles. Didn't they write much then?"
Mahogany child, son of arrivals on lower decks in chains,
sips distillation of cacao seeds, smirks at smiling mother
whose grandmothers sang to the chopping of cotton
so far from these canyons. A postcard to Detroit.
German couple honeymooning, coo on the veranda
over blue sky pool where children splash.

Orion already posed in the turquoise ether
could conceivably be a Comanche chief.

A Baptist preacher running for President
speaks of Rainbows.

Lee Schultz

FOND RECOLLECTIONS OF A FORMER FIRST LADY

Joe Betsy, James V. Allred's widow, smiled,
"Yes, I remember well that happy time —
Inauguration Day in '35 —
when Jimmy became governor of this state.
Our sons, a fourteen month old toddler, Dave,
and Jimmy, Jr., five, and I were dressed
in varied shades of blue. How proud I felt
when Jimmy introduced us to the crowd
of people gathered there to hear him speak.
The ball that night was held in four ballrooms.
An arm bouquet of roses matched my gown
and Jimmy stood so stately by my side.

It did not take us long to feel at home
within the mansion walls and spacious grounds.
A Texas Ranger guide and Margaret Mans
helped supervise our active little boys;
My grand piano was installed in my
bedroom, so I could practice every day.
A houseboy kept the mansion clean and served
the meals prepared by Clarence Chance who was
a splendid cook. Both men were trusties from
the Huntsville penitentiary. Those were
Depression days, so we grew vegetables
and flowers I arranged. We welcomed guests
like Mrs. Franklin Roosevelt who held
our newborn son, Sam Houston, in her arms.
We often entertained large groups of folks
and went on tours to publicize our state.

A bitter drouth prevailed and Texas was
a portion of the great dust bowl that plagued
our nation; but most farmers did survive.

My Jimmy was respected and well liked
for lasting contributions that he made
like old age pensions, setting up a Board
of Pardons and Paroles and Workman's Comp.
He was a true crusader and the people's friend."

Jennie Spray

MINI-PHOTOS OF MEMORIES

‘Remember Texas in 1936?" the old man asked —
and my mind's eye began to turn pages of years
backwards — backwards to Texas's 100th birthday.
Slowly, old black and whites of history flashed
back with mini-photos of that momentous time —
of CENTENNIAL time in Texas — and I remembered:

It was the year when Texans rediscovered their
roots — reremembered the Alamo, and Crockett,
Bowie, Travis — the Austins, Houston — when
they relived their historic past with pageantry
to commemorate the siege of Bexar, to recreate
the colorful saga of TEXAS UNDER SIX FLAGS.

It was the year that James V. Allred governed
the Lone Star, that Poet Laureate Grace Noll
Crowell lyricized her adopted State, that Texas's
own chronicler of tales, J. Frank Dobie, spiced
the columns of the *Fort Worth Press* with his de-
lectable centennial series, THE FLAVOR OF TEXAS.

It was the year we crisscrossed the State via
trains, or drove the family auto down two-lane
highways to Dallas's giant Central Expo and Cav-
alcade of Texas, to Fort Worth's panoramic West-
ern Frontier and Casa Mañana, to Mardi Gras and
Sun Carnivals, to Fiestas and Indian Ceremonials.

It was the year we listened to Roosevelt and
radio; danced to Juke Boxes and Big Bands;
walked miles of brilliant Midways housing memorabilia
and high tech; sneaked peeks at sideshows; rode
exhilarating rides; collected three cent commemora-
tive stamps and half-dollars; bought ten cent bread.

It was the year Texans temporarily forgot the
depressed Thirties, the rise of Germany's Hitler
and world turmoil amid fanfare and festivity,
amid pageantry of past, promise of tomor-
rows. It was a time for dreaming dreams as big
as the State itself. "It was a very good year!"

Ann Matthews Moorhead

TO A TREE BY A GRAVE

[*Dedicated to the people of New London, Texas, with thanks to Lynn Jackson.*]

Just another fella wanting to come up
and find out more about the explosion.

Questions like sawteeth come, one by one,
rake irreverently across smooth skin,
hunker down to the task at hand.
Bark tears like an old leather cover,
spills its sweet sap on ground long stained
with mounds of red dirt and tears.
Years, ring by ring, are laid open, exposed
like framed faces pulled from darkly
shelved corners.
Receding past Christmases
and Thanksgivings, past Fourths of July
and countless birthdays,
back to a bright new school remembered
now in clouds of dust.
The pith, bared,
stares forever on a rubble
of fallen dreams.

Into the other side now, swiftly,
the teeth sing old hymns remembered in east Texas
churches, tunes haunted by early spring shadows
of bent people and straight stone markers.
They rip old memories into again bright faces
leaning silently on still-young sorrows.
Ring by ring the tree resists, creaks,
and like something foreign, still stands
when the cutting is done.
The hush of its not falling is heard,
a quiet defiance against every trespassing sawyer,
every prying tooth.

C. J. Wells

1938

A SENSATIONAL TEXAS POLITICIAN

Swinging his shoulders, tapping his toes
to fiddles, guitars and banjos,
"Pappy" W. Lee O'Daniel came stepping into fame
with a hillbilly band, a million radio fans
and a flair for selling flour.
Famous for mountain music and his line,
"The Light Crust Doughboys are on the air,"
he was the LOVE of the Texas countryside,
for he could set hands to clapping, feet to stomping
with that hillbilly swing.

One day in nineteen thirty-eight,
a blind man said, "RUN FER GOV'NER, PAPPY!"
But the flamboyant O'Daniel's interest was flour,
"big fluffy white biscuits" . . . NOT POLITICS,
NOT till he gazed at that gorgeous rose granite
Capitol, its great dome glistening
beneath a Texas sky; then folks heard him swear,
    "Yeah man, I'll go for the Governor's Chair!
    Them hillbillies are politicians now!"

When the BIGWIGS heard that, they laughed
in his face, ha! ha! ha-ing, calling him names:
Hillbilly Hick! A flimflam flour man from Podunk!"
But O'Daniel was a man with million dollar dreams,
a country boy grown tall, good at corncob fights.
He leapt into the race like a hound after a jackrabbit,
met the city slicker BIGWIGS face to face, telling 'em,
    "Them hillbillies are politicians now!"

When he came round the mountain in a sound truck,
swinging to the fiddles of his Hillbilly Boys,
folks greeted him with shoe boxes of fried chicken,
pies, kisses and hugs, filling his flour barrels
with dollars and dimes,
lovin' his talk of better times.

AND WHEN HE WON, there was dancing! Hats flying!
News lines hummed, across the USA,
calling "PAPPY" W. LEE O'DANIEL the most sensational
politician in Texas history. He gazed again
at that gorgeous rose granite Capitol;
then he spoke to the people,
    "You all come to see me! There'll be big doings!
    Bands, mountain hoedowns, buffalo barbecue!
    Them hillbillies are politicians now!"

Marjorie Burney Willis

TIMES OF TEXAS

Spring came as usual in '39, bluebonnets popping out all over
along the roads, paths, ditches and gullies.
The blue wave would bend in the wind
to welcome native and stranger alike.

Peaceful little towns and cities sitting on the wide open spaces
in '39, Texas stood at the crossroads:
go forward with ranch and farm expansion
or plunge into the trend to plan a different future.

Build factories, design tall buildings and live in mansions
Texas Almanac in '39 was telling in all copies they were selling.
All editions were soliciting many things
declaring this is the best, this costs less.

Dallas was doing most of the bragging
the best in everything, they were tagging.
Dallas, First City in the world to have a Medical Arts Building,
WFAA largest, best now, 50,000 watts, ya hear?

Cowboys and cows were really invented in Texas
as was bragging, branding, bullriding and calf roping.
Rail lines were king, the way to go!
Down in Austin, The Driskill charged no extra for radio music in the room.

Many Texans said it was so that Chicago was closer to Texarkana than was El Paso.
Big hunt was on for oil and gas, the Hunt boys doing a lot of hunting.
Texas oil fields were pumping gas and black Texas gold like no end in sight.

Houston, magic town, long ago began turning things around.
They thought about taking the town to the sea.
But Galveston was already there,
decided it was easier to bring the sea to Houston.

From the crowded streets of old San Antone
to the cowboy that rode the range alone
Texans were proud and happy in '39,
proud of their past, bullish on the future, sure all would be well.

In Fort Worth, the undeclared war with Dallas was still white hot.
Dallas was east and Fort Worth west.
Each declared that they were the best.
Hated to see '39 end, but that old year sure did set a powerful trend.

Larry Rankin

VI
Mainstream
1940–1986

Texas, during the last four decades of this era, became an industrial power in the American mainstream.

The war effort provided the base, and postponed demands sparked rapid growth following the war. Both people and industry moved to Texas. The people moved because they had become acquainted with Texas during their war service and liked it, while industry moved closer to an expanding market. One industry complemented another thus fostering growth. Further, the attitude of the people now encouraged the location of industrial plants in Texas. At the end of this period four out of five people lived in metropolitan areas.

Petroleum, with its lusty offspring the petrochemical industry, was dominant. But, the Oil Embargo of 1973 gave it a great shock and created uncertainties about the future which are still unresolved. Cotton, though still a major cash crop, is threatened by man-made fibers and foreign competition.

The petrochemical industry is unique to Texas and is its largest industry. It converts natural gas into a variety of products — synthetic rubber, plastics and industrial chemicals. Petrochemical plants are clustered so that products may be interchanged between processes.

The Space Program centered near Houston has encouraged growth. It created a sophisticated technology based on electronics, the silicon chip and exotic fuels. But, more than landing a man on the moon, and conquering space, the knowledge thus gained has been spun off to the benefit of earthbound products, new and improved.

A dark cloud hovers over future growth and that is the availability of water to support growth, a frontier yet to be conquered.

DEATH OF A MORNING

[For John F. Kennedy]

I

The morning

It must have been on such a morning God created Eve:
The soft November sun sang out the hills and fields,
And joy had come forever,
It was a time no man should be alone.

Yet in a nearby wood,
the yellow leaves poured down — poured down like tears;
And there were those who must have known,
Who surely must have known that even song must sometimes die
Of its own loveliness.

II

The moment

Through the soft November air, three shots rang out —
And in the falling of a leaf, the world exploded
With an awful truth.
A fearful darkness hid the sun. There was no morning anywhere —
No morning on this earth.

III

The man

Out of the quiet fact of Love, a man becomes.
He walks this spinning dust,
The stars above his breast, and inch by inch he moves
Toward the sun.

Such a man was this, our Chief:
A man of dignity and courage.
Intense and lovely and alive.

IV

The meaning

Did he foretell that fateful hour,
The final answer to his question:
What can I do for my Country?
Did he know, that Autumn dawn,
His last, long morning would grow old with history?

O world, believe:
There is no hate could dim that soft, November sun
that warmed his spirit.
Nor bullet ruin that young, green place within his heart.

Morning may die briefly with the breath,
But Light is never done.
O world, know this:
That Light is never done!

Libby Stopple

1940

THE SHIFTING BRAZOS

After supper,
in the minutes before a meeting at the schoolhouse,
W. Truman Brown, fisherman, sat alone on the wharf.
Alongside the battered boards
his shrimp boat nudged its moorings.
At the next pier his party boat, *Falcon II,* stood by
to carry sportsmen in search of marlin and redfish.
Beyond the river bend, blinking construction lights
marked the site where chemical magic would soon
extract magnesium from the sea.

Building that giant plant was changing everything.
All summer, huge trucks had lumbered through town,
growling at stop signs, raising ochre dusts.
Their raucous shifting of gears never stopped;
the dusts never settled. In front yards
silver trailer homes grew like toadstools.
A hotel had been raised up in seventeen weeks,
and at the telephone exchange the new hum
was Freeport talking to the world.
Brown no longer stopped at Chudly's barbershop
for Saturday coffee. Chud was always busy,
his hands shuttling above unknown faces.

Tonight's session, grappling new bond issues
and municipal offices, would be long, uncharted.
He lit a cigarette. The spent match
hit the water lightly and scooted
through the swirl at the piling.
Tugging at the short bill of his fisherman's cap,
Mayor Brown started for the schoolhouse.

Conrad W. Marvin

1941

BASTION BUILT

"Sargeant stone," we said, "local, to hold the same,
With hill men to break and lay it so." Highland still,
Caught, culled to keep secure in rock and cedar brake.
No lack here, though verged to wage so vast a war.
That for outside and bastion built.

At heart within, to frame central flame and warmth
For all, these strong-drawn figures in tile, Pilgrim
They are. Still intent with ship and sail, their come
And go. All hued in dusky brown as keyed for war.
So this house is rock bound as any North Sea highland.

Thus pilgrim at heart, harbors its fire in every tone
Of flame and glow that never can be quenched. For that,
Thank you, Lionel Barrymore, two-hand to bind, hold fast
Through and on out beyond any unhorizoned war
Or universal, whether land or water.

Fair share and sequel with its granite State House.
Local as cut, laid, built. Its ancestral Highlanders,
Its Pilgrims for their common at-heart epitome:
Snow white and winged to overview, keep guard
For freemen to build, hold aloft its living flame.

Allie Merle Dunaway

JUDSON THRASH

The willows sit yet like boys, dangling their feet
in the shaded water,
brink-lovers, tenants of the edge, neither of the land
nor of the river,
much as he was. April or August, he would come and
patiently set out his pole.
Then slump against a trunk to watch his cork, breasting
the sluggish current:
sit thus for half the day, not much concerned if some
stray perch
or unseen lazy catfish tugged haphazardly at the bait.
He had no quarrel with fish, nor with water, nor
with anything.
No melancholy, no philosophy. But what he did, he did.

He had a kinship with these ways. The blood moved in
his veins
slow, soberly, as the dull red Brazos water;
his, the soul of the green turtle, basking on a naked log.
The mind in him, the human attribute, had a laborious spread,
a scope and far-off sweep, a soaring, unproductive flight
like the skimming buzzard's, buoyed on the twisting wind,
hoping to dip for occasion. Yet a reptilian reluctance,
a sense of withdrawal, the odor of stone, the deep
burrow, the ledge.

That they took him from this milieu, think for yourself
the predicate.
Bitter, or comic, or tragic, whatever is befitting.
He had no quarrel with Jap, nor with German, nor anyone.
The end of it only was likely: there in the stagnant delta,
by the wide Irrawaddy. It was much as here on the Brazos
when the boys with their .22 rifles, seeing the surfacing turtle
surprise the dull, stupid beak. And the punctured shell gushes red,
tinging the water. And the whole heavy bulk shudders and
slowly submerges.

William D. Barney

TEXAS CONTRIBUTES

This middle year of war we live
in Honey Grove. It's peaceful here, although
I rehearse each day for combat overseas
with neighboring Camp Maxey's khaki hordes.
The infantry division training here
is one of twenty major fighting teams
all Texas will help build. Some women soldiers
invade our olive drabness. They reflect
the grace and style of Texan Colonel Hobby.

This year once-quiet Texas has become
the U.S. Army's largest training ground,
and with its more than forty airfields,
the free world's greatest year-round training sky.

Allied forces in the Mediterranean
are winning under General Ike. In Honey Grove
our neighbors say he came from Denison,
and that the Admiral of the U.S. Fleet,
Pacific, Chester Nimitz, was born and reared
in Fredericksburg. No news has surfaced yet
of Commander Sam Dealey, Dallas sailor,
or teenaged Audie Murphy, Farmersville soldier.
Their bravery will soon be writing legends.

This year another Texan, named Tom Connally,
writes the Senate Resolution that affirms
the U.S.A. will join, postwar, to build
an international body to preserve world peace.

Since '39, before Pearl Harbor was attacked,
Texans have been enlisting here at home
or signing up in Canada, allied
to help crush Hitler, to restore world peace,
believing, as Texans always have,
that the answer to moral confusion
can sometimes be straight action.

Kimo Dunn

1944

TEXAS: NINETEEN HUNDRED FORTY-FOUR

'Twas the year nineteen hundred forty-four and Texans were still in war,
Some were in Europe, and the Pacific which seemed so very far,
June 6, "D-Day-Operation Overlord," the battle for Normandy began,
A Texan, General Dwight D. Eisenhower, was made Allied Command.
Admiral Chester W. Nimitz, had the Japanese navy sail for land.
Battles in Europe and Pacific left memories not soon forgot,
And many a soldier was left on land and in the sea to rot.
War Bonds were sold to help pay for World War II,
Prayers were given in churches that the war would soon be through.
Homes had become like hotels, mostly a place to sleep,
Members were on a work schedule which was very hard to keep.
We regret to inform you, were the saddest a family received,
Crying and moaning filled many a home that was grieved.
Rationing, points and tokens were a part of daily life,
And many an article was rationed to help in the sacrifice.
In the halls of congress were able Texas men:
Vice-President John Nance Garner, known as "Cactus Jack,"
Gave us the FDIC to protect depositors when bank money was gone,
Had already retired to Uvalde which was his beloved home.
Representative Sam Rayburn, gave us the Truth-in-Securities Act,
The REA, the FCC, and was "Mr. Speaker" with tact.
Senator Tom Connally gave the resolution for our nation to be in UNO,
To promote unity among nations, and men wherever they would go.
Senator W. Lee O'Daniel, known as "Pappy," left his aura
As governor with his platform of the Ten Commandments,
And his song, *Beautiful, Beautiful, Texas,* ringing in the land.
Representative Lyndon Baines Johnson's day had not fully come,
His wide expanse of civil rights as president, was yet to be done.
Governor Coke R. Stevenson brought fiscal responsibility to the state,
And through his legislation sought to make her great.
A few lines cannot tell the greatness of the Lone Star State,
Neither can one year on the calendar of time make her rate.
Only in the mind, the heart, and the deeds of her people,
Stretched across the years of history, recorded in time,
Will we find her greatness this sesquicentennial, in the rhyme
Of our state song, *Texas Our Texas,* "So wonderful! So great."

Weems S. Dykes

1945

DEATH OF A PRESIDENT

Four years had passed, four long years
Since you spoke the words that shocked a nation:
"This is a day that will live in infamy."
In the grim aftermath of war,
Shaken by the slaughter of tens of thousands,
Your great heart finally gave out.
You had brought comfort and hope
In the fireside chats and the many speeches
That rivalled those of your friend Churchill.
Your voice had spoken eloquently
For the cause of peace around the world.
In this year, 1945, you were laid to rest,
With all the accolades that could be given
By a grateful nation to its chief.
I offer my sprig of lilac too;
I was eleven years old when I heard the news
From a weeping mother who adored you.
The words she said were simple enough:
"Son, a great man was laid to rest today,
And you must never forget
That he lived and died for Liberty."
Mother is dead now too,
But the lesson remains within my heart
And I will tell it to my children too,
Because we loved the patriot soul in you.

John D. Vaughan

1946

WAR BRIDE

Bridget Becket Smith boarded the *Queen Mary*
loaded with 1700 war brides and children,
waved goodbye to her native Welshland,
and sailed for the Lone Star State.

She was welcomed by a swaggering cowhand
with jingling spurs, chaps,
and wide-brimmed Stetson.
Her husband, ex-GI, Johnny L. Smith
was a real true cowboy.
His artificial limb fitted securely
into the scuffed leather boot.
She was awed by the picturesque ranch
extending in every direction,
and loved the lifestyle of roping, branding,
bronchobusting, square dancing, rancheros.

Together, they toured the beautiful state
from plains to mountains to seashores,
savoring the vastness of its wealth and beauty.
Oil wells pumping ribbons of greenish-black gold
were a never ceasing wonder,
but most of all she liked the warmth
of friendly, handshaking people.

Summer nights were magical dreams
when the moon swung low in its hammock,
coyotes yowled a serenade,
and stars, like eyes, round and bright
dripping with luster.

Now, she knew why Johnny bragged so much
and felt a swell of pride to bear his name.
Like so many transplanted war brides
she learned to love her adopted state,
and boasted as proudly as any native
in her newly-acquired Texas drawl.

Mrs. R. E. (Lou) Gatlin

1947

WHAT PRICE?

as if there weren't enough trouble that year
Texas City blew up in April, explosions
that killed hundreds, injured thousands
flying
above the smoke, a World War II correspondent
was reminded of Nagasaki obliterated by *the bomb* . . .
an omen? an arrow pointed toward tomorrow?
in March, Harry Truman had stood before Congress
and, naming no names, launched the Cold War

but editors placed the rift with Russia second
behind the high cost of living when they voted
on the top ten stories of the year
for butter
had gone to a dollar a pound, milk was selling
for twenty-three cents, bread for six,
good homes? fifteen to thirty-five thousand dollars

that fall there were meatless, eggless, poultryless days
even though sugar rationing had ended in June

yet Tomball, Texas, boasted it had the lowest
living costs in the United States: there
a man could rent a lovely brick home
for fifty dollars a month, including free
gas and water, a restaurant lunch cost
forty- to forty-five cents, a hamburger
only fifteen . . .

there is a poetry of prices

we all have to learn
what things cost:

the price we pay for bread

the price we pay for peace

the price we pay for love

most of all,
for love . . .

Gene Shuford

VOTING IN JIM WELLS COUNTY

In the Mexican precinct
In George Parr's country,
They do not come out often.
But now, so bored with death,
The loneliness of topsoil so heavy upon them
They eagerly come forth
Into the light again,
To be heard
As they have not for so long a time.

Determined ghosts, they rise
To be counted,
Not in Last Judgement
But by how they themselves judge.
Voting for L.B.J., all of them,
They outnumber the stuffed ballot boxes
For Stevenson in Houston's River Oaks.

Then, fatigued by the effort
They retire, pass like shadows
Into their graves again,
Awaiting the next time
The dead can make a difference.

Christopher Woods

1949

THE ICE STORM

Between contractions
my mother dreamed
of black water,
a lake by a road
I fell in and fell in.
She'd reach shoulder deep,
feel my small hand slipping
down and away
and startle awake to the
hospital radiator
crackling its spine,
the crazed wind glazing
everything.

So I was born wet and cold,
my cradle tipped
by an iced howl
I never forgot.

On the edge of the Caprock,
where the prairie drops
its glacial face to a
warm, rolling south,
I wrapped frozen pipes
while a deer carcass creaked
from the wellhouse rafters,
creaked and swung its
bloodied shoulders
against my breath.
The sights of my 12-gauge
held miles of prairie;
held the alert, empty
eye thoughts of rabbits;
held the buried light
of Cherokee flint;
held the fast hearts
of wintered sparrows.
And the sky's mouth held
my grandmother's life
waiting to happen;
my mother's life
waiting to happen;
my sister's life
waiting to happen —
thawless, grinding
the edge of the Caprock.

When the Great Storm of '62
closed the school early
I tramped the miles home
through ice-stubbled acreage
and cut ice from
the door with a hoe.

Inside, the rooms
were chilled brittle,
waiting.

I huddled with a pot
of bitter coffee,
braced, pushed
and dropped out of childhood.

Charles Behlen

1950

JUSTICE FOR ALL

Complacent in their ignorance,
Texans pulled their prejudice over their minds
and answered the pollsters.
They confirmed their opposition to human rights,
and the world read that 76% of them favored segregation
and would deny blacks the right to attend white colleges.
In November they elected Allan Shivers, a segregationist,
and would have been content to live with others
in their shadow,
but the Supreme Court changed things in 1950.
The court banned segregation in interstate transportation,
and the "separate but equal" facilities
at the new Houston airport
became equal without separation.
The court also ruled for Heman Sweatt,
A black man who sought to enter
The University of Texas Law School.
He entered the school in September of 1950
along with others for whom he had opened the door.
Walls were falling, attitudes changing.
Texans discovered they were many colors, of many beliefs.
The candle flickered in the vast darkness,
but persisted.
Illumination was long past due,
but in 1950
there were new reasons for hope,
new dreams of what could be.

Budd Powell Mahan

COWGIRL

yes i was a cowgirl
living outside san antonio
on a military reservation
the year begun with chinese fire
in korean skies
and you can bet i saw 7000
recruited young men
who moved into tents down the street
from my daddy-the-captain's quarters
january cold front and not enough supplies
my daddy said for so many men
not enough fuel for their tent fires and
from the school bus windows i watched them
swinging arms and legs together
calling out their rhymes
breath cold white

but fire of palominos
in the springtime
fiesta de los caballos
and you better believe i was a cowgirl
got the plastic yellow fringe
on snazzy vest and short-pants
my mama sewed for me
pre-pubescent vamp-of-texas style
(boots next year my daddy promised)
palominos lead all parades in san antonio
city of horses prancing
past ten-year-old cowgirls
lining the sidewalks
while someonc is dreaming
of fire soon-to-be
in palomino stables
soon-to-consume palominos
too frenzied to gallop through flames
gala parade palominos

yes wasn't it only a dream
that fire would eat horses and men
up so soon?
burned horseflesh singed hair blowing
already through Gateway of Air
and all of its Forces
but i was only a cowgirl
yearning for boots next year
dreaming of creamy gold horses

Pat Ellis Taylor

1952

FROM BRENHAM TO HOUSTON

The poker lamp cast angled amber on their faces,
Cigar smoke floating beneath.
They had fallen silent, eyes locked,
Fingertips drumming the Brenham Inn tablecloth.
August breeze curled around the old window shades
Gently lifting their collars, swinging bolo ties.
Crumpled cracker cellophane rolled across the floor.

A covered wagon for Pete's sake! From Brenham to Houston?
Mayor Reese Lockett shifted in his seat.
Never had he seen so much brass in one room.
Ad man Charlie Geizendanner.
Channel 2 in full force — Jack Harris, Pat Flaherty.
PR for the Fat Stock Show & Rodeo!? . . . Welllllll . . .
Ping!
Tobacco hitting the spittoon echoed like a pistol shot.
Lockett looked at two faces in the corner, weathered like trusty leather.
Emil Marks and John Warnash, cowmen from way back —
With them at the reins it might work.
Chair feet scraped wood as he slapped Charlie on the back.
"Gentlemen, let's try it!"

They climbed in the wagon one February morn so dank
The sky looked like campfire smoke,
Horses stomping, steaming in the chill.
Ho!
Off they went, bits, beer and teeth rattling down 290,
Flaherty hugging his TV mike like a june bug on a porch light.
He told the story in detail — towns, trees, clouds, churches —
Transmitted through air in Houston.
Main Street was lined three throng when the wagon clattered into town,
Men breaking barriers to ask if they could ride along next year.
Children perched on shoulders,
Squealing as the horses hopped and shimmied through the clamor.

With ears ringing Lockett raised his eyes to the top of Esperson,
Fine mist dampening the brim of his Stetson.
"Good Lord, I don't believe it!"
The Salt Grass Trail Ride was born.

Lynn Carol Reynolds

1953

IN RETROSPECT

This is KUHT Houston.
On this final day of 1953, let's take a look
at some of the events that made news in Texas.

This year saw President Eisenhower bringing home
many of our men by effecting a truce in Korea.
Those who stayed home engaged in other battles.
Senator Price Daniel led the fight to restore the
tidelands to the states.
Spanish law prevailed and we won the right to
three leagues of submerged coastal lands.

Our normal "unusual" weather was much in the news.
A drouth created acute water shortages for farmers
and ranchers. Eisenhower responded to Governor Allan
Shivers by granting federal aid.
Devastating tornadoes hopscotched through the
state leaving death and destruction — Waco
suffered the most serious assault.

I would have to rate as top story of the year this
TV station signing on as the first educational channel
in the nation! Charged exhilaration pulsed through
my being as I began beaming knowledge to unknown
receivers. I felt a sudden kinship with the one for
whom this city was named. The thirst for adventure
and quest for enlightenment led Sam Houston to his
rendezvous with history. Perhaps I, too, will
be linked to some spectacular unbelievable
event yet to come.

Wrapping up the year, I would say that we feel
good about ourselves!
The war in Korea is over, the tidelands have been
secured and we are rebuilding our damaged areas.
This is the news voice of KUHT leaving you with this
thought — bighearted, flamboyant and reckless Texas
rushes out to meet the future — the
challenger and the challenged!

Marie R. Fleming

A CURVE IN THE ROAD

It was a curve in the road
with an upward slope,
a turning point
from any point of view,
the hinge of the century, 1954,
slightly off center
to balance the door to the future.

I remember the year — if I may be pardoned —
I traded industry for a profession
and gained an immediate associate
when my son returned from Korea.
World War II had dropped on Texas,
in lieu of bombs,
military camps and personnel,
igniting massive matrimony
and a popcorn explosion
of precious new souls.
The song of saws and ring of hammers,
for nine years since Nagasaki,
had reached a zenith
and the baby boom
was graduating from kindergarten.

Austin, the Capital,
had come of age,
maturing from a country town
to a city of metropolitan ilk.
The State fell in line
and closed ranks
with the Nation.

Cecil L. Child

1955

SIX, TWENTY-THREE, FIFTY-FIVE

[*Death of Amon G. Carter, Sr.*]

Young summer was chilled when the Pale Horse
galloped into Cowtown and its rider said
"I have come for Amon."
Words froze on penpoints. Printing presses choked.
As airways blazoned the news,
a whisper of sadness encircled his Lone Star Domain —
"Our Amon is dead."
Death gnawed the ropes and the curtain crashed
on Amon's one-man Western Show staged in wealth and luxury,
spending and splurging, benevolence and ballyhoo —
a flamboyant empire to shame Caesar and outflame Nero.
Manna for hungry eyes and music for listening ears;
Amon's words of faith, hope and fun had flown from his
newspaper nest to an eager, waiting West,
telling it who, what and why it was forever the best.
Horn tooter. Pistol shooter. West rooter.
You diademmed the cowboys, Levied the queens,
held hands with royalty, ate beans
with peasants and presidents and corralled celebrities.
Maverick Monarch of more than you surveyed who
lassoed national attention and rodeoed into universal mention.
Death, you have his body in a marble vault, but
Amon, we have your spirit in a marble museum,
floored with enduring mosaics,
walled with Remingtons and Russells and
roofed with big Texas Stars.
He did not die on the vine but pruned it to
perennial fruiting with cowboy hat, chaps and a sixer —
riding a fiery Pegasus into an embracing West.
Cheating poverty and obscurity, you nickled and dimed
a stairway to millions, then tossed them into a whirlwind of
pioneering, publishing, making and taking, but over all —
giving.
And to your last question, "Am I still here?"
we simply reply,
"Yes, Amon, . . . YOU ARE STILL HERE."

Guy Malone

1956

WHERE ARE THE PIONEERS?

Where have they gone, the pioneers,
who rode the hills in former years,
who freighted with their burro trains
in mountain trails and winding lanes
between the pines and junipers
who trapped the streams for beaver furs?
For food in wilderness for brave men
of rabbit, jerky and sage hen,
where did they go these many years
with all their laughter and their tears?
On a hilltop now one can see
lonely graves marked in memory.
We cannot say, just who now lies
in unkept graves beneath the skies.
Perhaps they are the pioneers
who paid their tributes and arrears
with all they had, and now lie prone
without a marker or a stone.

Gladyse Bryan Carrico

1957

CONFRONTATION

Dallas 1957

They're saying the Devil himself came.
Out of the South flying low
He collided with an Easter
Cold front moving full tide
Toward the big bend in the Mexican border.
Reeling out of the blackening squall
the prince of darkness
spiraled down and
out of the clouds
in a short-lived
stinging reign
of deafening
fury, a
flailing
topsy-turvy
sidewinding
cornucopia of
lightning
black
mud
and
hail.

Cold eyes blazing, he left
Ten funerals, several baptisms.
Acres of new parking, and enough
Homespun yarns
To make a few new old-timers
Spin forever.

Ken Hammes

THE BIRTH OF A POET

After the earlier droughts comes the time for a good crop:
I see in the green and white with the light gold of the sun
Shining that fall in the cotton that I too felt the Doubt
That brings Belief. There in Anson, a poet is born, a star
Of the mind of men, a believer in the Truth of Women, and
What they can bring in the ways that they bring them.
So that now in these years of General Failure, Technique
Takes control, questioning the Existential Nature of Man,
Making a Big Deal of the Whole Thing. (I mean All. I don't
Mean a Little Bit.) The Broad Notion is that we are generally
Here for some specific *REASON*. Our lovers here are one way
We deal with all that Spiritual Ecstasy, however we derive its
Benefits. *OUR MISSION HERE IS OUR MISSION HERE STOP*

O believe now the folded fire tongue of the pentecostal
Coastland, the joy of the whooping crane, whooping it up,
The mating dance, the jumping up and down in the water,
The light splash white of the sunlight on the marsh grass
Before all goes orange — Sure, I been down in the valley,
And the oranges there still the tip of my tongue!

Wanting Truth and not Justice, Greg Glazner grows up in Anson,
Where the old courthouse silver Justice holds her scales in one
Hand, sword in the other; her blindfold, silver too like the rest
Of her in a time of needed gold. Becoming the boy poet,
Differentiating the outside from the inside, yellow hair grows
On his towhead. Becoming the man poet, he goes off to Montana
To learn the Extent, the Breadth and Height of that West Texas Sky.
Having been Here and There, not the first man to walk two landscapes,
He is perhaps the first to put his foot down — a lenient step for
Mankind! Learning everything there was to learn from the masters,
Becoming masterful himself, he knows that knowing is not enough.

He begins over again, because there is no place else to start:
Let us not depart   from the art of the heart,
For there is no other part   like a Metaphysical Art,
And no other Thing like a Human, and no other Human like a Poet.

Larry D. Griffin

1959

THE FIFTIES FINALE!

The end of the fifties saw such growth
From Panhandle to Gulf shore.
But we're the biggest state there is,
So, howdy, folks, there's room for more!

The scene is Austin? Three called sessions!
Low revenues gave no pleasure.
What'll we tax? Teachers need money . . .
Is a sales tax the right measure?

"No, suh!" the hue and cry was heard
From each part of the State.
We can't have *that* tax just yet.
Low taxes make Texas great!

And north of Austin, "Mayor Dallas"
For a fourth term was elected.
Ole Bob Thornton gave them pride
With blessings for Dallas selected.

The easier pace of the fifties ended
And changes were coming fast.
Magnolia became Mobil Oil.
Won't even the Red Horse last?

Then the news came from Washington . . .
What happened some thought 'most a sin.
We were no longer the largest state
For they let Alaska in!

But Texas pride withstood the blow
Of no more the biggest in land;
As we found it was the people's warmth
Which had made our State so grand!

Barbara Farnell

SITTING ON A GRANITE ROCK

Old Texas worked his way along the granite jetties
over one boulder, then another
until he and the Gulf were face to face.

He lay his tackle box,
his rod and reel to the side, carefully,
so as not to lose them
to some grinning whitecap
breaking to run along the rocks.

HE SAT BROODING

The last decade puzzled —
a great state restlessly sleeping
the call to space
the fiery energy churning in his chest.
A dissatisfaction of spirit
an ancient yearning
and the children —
what was upheaving the children?

That young squirt television
was going to have to be dealt with.
He had listened to those two bright men.
He wasn't sure it hadn't
elected a president.

And now there was Lyndon.
No two in the nation.
Son-of-a-gun!

He pulled his old salty hat
down over his forehead,
baited his hook,
cast it expertly
landing it seventy feet out
deep into the forming fume
of the great society.

Mickey Huffstutler

1961

OUR CAMELOT

I recall this innocent year of Camelot.
We had a gallant First Family, a New Frontier,
a Peace Corps, and . . . *Ask not what your country*
    can do for you . . .
An idealistic year. But I wonder
if those Knighted Brothers were pawns in its plot
to enchant us and camouflage its fires?

Vietnam was quietly smouldering.
Oswald was scheming in the Soviet.
Russia was using psychic craft
    to whisper away our courage.
Gagarin rocketed into space ahead of Alan
    Shepard who would later walk on the moon.

Martin's faith was overcoming hate.
But the Berlin Wall set hate in concrete
and wire. As if to say, "Faith
can't tear hate down."

Texas polished her stars: Republican Tower
became United States Senator.
Lyndon took over as Vice-President but he
would wear the poisoned laurel. In November
Rayburn died, not knowing Dallas's horror.

1961, you were, indeed, a fabled year . . .
But was a fairy tale the best that you could do?

Katrin E. Schoonmaker

THE COLD CAME HARD

A man flew to the moon
while we watched from the icy ground.

The cold came hard that January,
icy moonlit nights
and days hardly warmer.

The cold came hard that January,
pouring down from the Plains,
running icy fingers over Texas citrus,
closing streets, stores, schools.

The cold came hard that January.
The young expectant mother left her heater on,
so the family's Christmas puppy would not freeze.

The fire started from the furnace.
When she came back, there was
only a smoldering ruin
and firemen standing helplessly by.

Her children were safe, her husband was safe,
so when she collapsed in the ice and snow
she wept for a tiny black dog.

And the firemen could not say,
"He's dead. See, here in the box? We saved his cold body for you."
So they went away as the young mother wept . . .
and in a corner of the icy yard
moonlight and snow
fell on the puppy's cold, black body.

The cold came hard that January.

Theresa Horton Waller

ONCE UPON A TIME IN DALLAS

Just a pleasant autumn day it seemed to be,
That day in Dallas in nineteen sixty-three . . .

But how will Dallas be remembered
When they roll back its history's bitter scroll?
November, and still the day was mild,
The grass still green upon a nearby knoll,

(A place where some would see conspiracy).
Spectators filled a parklike esplanade,
Some spilling past the curbs in eagerness
To watch their leader in his motorcade.

Then a cry, "They're coming!" and there he was,
In spite of warning, in an open car,
Head bare, waving, smiling, a true Sir Lancelot,
Who, meeting Cuba's threat, stalled off a war.

Ignoring danger, he kept the openness
He wanted with the people, and trusted luck,
His Lady by his side, the day so bright.
No shadows here — and then the bullets struck.

His head jerked back, then forward from the force.
Blood fountained. His wife screamed, reached out to him.
Then each action seemed turned to slow motion,
Like nightmare, or a scene from some stopped film.

The crowd, stunned out of joy, stood bewildered.
Bodyguards swarmed the car, their powers
Useless now. The governor, too, was fallen.
The woman's crawl backward for help took hours.

The front of her pink suit was soaked with blood,
A sight that goaded the startled crowd to run,
Some for safety, some with screams of horror,
A few pointing up where light struck a gun.

In seconds the car leaped forward, speeding him
Out of their lives, out of their world. Brief, brief
His time with them. Yet time enough for love to grow,
Time enough to hone the cruel blade of grief.

Just a pleasant autumn day it seemed to be,
That day in Dallas in nineteen sixty-three . . .

Virginia Long

THE TALE OF TWO SCORE AND TWENTY FOUR

On the eve of escape
from the timber and soil
Into the clutches of steel and mortar;
Under the hands of poverty
And the feet of lingering
disenfranchisement —
A new society lurched.
'Twas the Great One
of LBJ
in the shadow of the Act
of '64;
'Twas the mystical strength
of hovering enfranchisement
for the minor kinds;
AND the aura of other
emblems of progress
for these ethnic types.

'Twas remnants from a
separate and unequal
educational system for the
development of minor, ethnic
Texana;
And the haunt of removal
of the Big Government's
Support . . .
That told the Tale of
Two Score and Twenty-Four.

Patricia A. R. Williams

THE SAME MOON

It was the same moon
That led high-hearted pioneers
    across the Texas plains,
That washed the Davis mountains in pale glow
And brought forth whispered tales
    of white buffalo, lost love, and treachery,
That glittered shifting sand dunes
    by Padre's cresting waves,
Made the tall Karankawa
    lie restless in their graves.

But in this year,
Small man-creatures leapfrogged
    across its troubled face,
And in this year,
It shadowed youthful figures
Moving cautiously onto an alien Asian shore,
As far from home, it seemed,
As those who traveled miles through space.

While back in Texas,
A tall and lonely man
With worry wrinkles etched deep into his brow,
Pondered these things,
Looked out across the moonwashed Pedernales tide —
And sighed.

Zinita Fowler

MAJOR ARCANUM: THE TOWER

[*For him, for her, for them. d. August 1, 1966*]

Somewhere
somewhere between the sword's point of Now
and the wailing wall of historical Present,
somewhere between the Yahweh-eye of Sun
and Time's shellprints on overtrodden stone,

When
when heat's wavings verticaled and surged,
stroking the turgid rage of rigid Tower,
when quadruple Clock bronzed out foreverly
that unheard, un-to-be remembered Noon,

Over
over the broken Words, fetched from afar,
over the gilded shards of shattered alphabets,
over the wailing wall of hysterical Present,
resolved at last, he thrust the sword of Now.

Later
Later, for them for whom there is no later,
an Austin moon alighted with a silver shriek
freezing onto overtrodden stones, into Memoriam,
their unseen, un-to-be-forgotten Blood.

Fritz Hensey

ON ONE QUIET BUS RIDE

[*The author was riding from Laredo to San Antonio to begin his basic military training, his first trip away from home.*]

On one quiet bus ride
in 1967
Texas outgrew my Laredo. it stretched
beyond the faces of those border guards and
rusted *rio grande* waters
beyond familiar dusts of barrio people or
aromas of *carne guisada*, hot coffee and tortillas
to the nervous words of LBJ:
eight sad days into this new year
and killed are a hundred and forty-four —
wounded, countless more

and in the soundless passing of mesquite trees, huisaches,
nopales and telephone poles
Texas grows. it sits on the deathbed of Jack
the other Jack
who made an illegal turn behind a Dallas bus
and wound up parked on Oswald's face
Jack's dead
and the year is young

my face is plastered to the tinted window
somewhere between Cotulla and Pearsall
as cattle eat seared cactus and dry grass
Texas grows. it kneels by five catholic priests
in the back of a pickup truck
on their way to jail for defending farmworkers
the battles are on
and it's only the first of February

by August universities will be ant hills of defiance; a state
law will make it a crime to bury Blacks and Chicanos
alive; and a slice of El Paso will be returned to Diaz Ordaz
while Texas grows
more than it can boast

Jose Flores Peregrino

THE GOOD A MAN DOES

[. . . *March 31, 1968 — a day that I profoundly hoped would mark the beginning of the end of the war that had brought so much pain and anguish to the people of my country.*

— Lyndon Johnson]

What is the good those in power can't undo?
When by tens and dozens the bags are filled, zipped,
and loaded, then piled in slumps of plump black dew,
to be slipped back home by dark of plane and ship?
The evil that they did, these valiant men,
uproots by thatches of white crosses, by crotch
of granite rock, acres of unburied hatchets
aimed at the unopened sky which continued
to rain light and fire onto huts of silence.
At last, Johnson too wanted rest from the night,
From Tet, to go home, and call a bombing halt,
Ready to leave behind a nation to face his country.
In us, Texas, somewhere we proudly prepared
that fallen year of heavy rain and war to accept
our son home, fresh from failure, wrapped and geared
in the robes of the native elderly — Lyndon noble, defeated,
half-retired, relaxed to the rural sway
of homeland drought, the dry vigor of hope
falling by the wayside: "I wanted to heal
some of those wounds and restore unity . . ." But
Within four days King lay dead; in months, Kennedy —
Then the long summer of dissolution, Nixon,
Iran, Reagan, other discomfitting, uncomforted words.
Can any Texan's country peace resist a breaking war?
The peace of age waited to bloom alone
Beside the Pedernales, breathing in retreat
Over the slow, restless waters beneath fists
Of cloud and swarms of bees. "I wanted to comfort her,"
He said, "and I could not," consoling a daughter
Whose husband had returned to Saigon. Whenever
His calm swerved into the Red Room, he stopped
Before Wilson "stretched out upstairs in the White House,
Powerless to move, the machinery of American government
In disarray around him . . ." A war behind him, too.
Lyndon home from the Hill, so pitched to roll
And sputter in released freedom, nagged by the nation's heart:
"Why, she asked, was her husband going away to fight? . . .
I wanted to comfort her and I could not."

Michael Ditmore

1969

TRANSITIONAL TEXAS

In it came with a practical ring
A wintery feeling that would turn to spring.
Solid and friendly; to the world benign
To Texans, a transitional '69.

But it was people, this year of date
Struggling for meaning and being; to rate.
Who waxed in words, of anger sown
And pushed for power, for being known.

Was it politician, student, and womankind
Or black, brown, red, and white, blind
Whose frustrated incomprehension added to the flow
And provided an ally to the foe.

Yet another person, so tall to see
With shoulders strong, broad and free
Steady eyes, and strong of hand
Had placed a magic on the land.

Who stood the test of sectarian strife
And placed a value on human life.
Who rose to heights with ideologies sought
And treasured achievements, mightily fought.

Who with steady vision bright
Set an anchor for stately might.
With peace for all, above a claim
For fettered power and fostered fame.

Who, with friend and compadre, it's plain to say
Provided another transitional day.
Who stepped aside, that peace prevail
And woe to all, if that should fail.

For transitions made are sometimes prime
And achievements stand the test of time
For plans from dreams, and congeniality
Flight in space, a reality.

For softly as the fluttering of a mockingbird
The Spirit of Friendship again has been heard.
On the sands of the moon, haughtily standing
The giant *Eagle* has made its landing.

This was a year that was meant to be
The Lone Star, echoing, for all to see
Strong, friendly, transitional Texas
A state in a land that's free.

Jerry L. Preas

COLORS

red and green;
Christmas colors
fertilize spring's grass
with student's blood
from Kent State and Jackson State

white and black;
Easter shades without
resurrection;
the headlines tell of new
colors at UT and UH — black
banded arms drop the flag
half-staff against an
ashen sky.

blue and gray;
winter hues ring in the death
cries; symbols only mourn
official heroes: hoist the
stained flag to its proper
height —
"O Say Can You See . . ."

light and dark;
"O yes I can see . . .
the betrayal of an era;"
the generation of light that
became lost in the
dark green and gold of the
American Dream.

red and green;
bricks and lawns . . .
a fitting suburban memorial
for the death of hope.

Teresa McDonald Cortez

1971

THE SENTINEL

Hail to the Chief.
Hear civilized, measured applause
To the President who was and to the one
Who will not be.
Pride absent of foreboding shame.
The helicopter nearby wants to silence
The clamor of nature this morning in May.
A marble mausoleum
Shoots into the brillant sky
Weighty with dead life.

Overlooking the Great Hall   four stories high
Enclosed by the Great Wall   bulletproof glass
Remembering the War   the one we lost,
Identical red boxes with the gold Presidential seal
Stand. The mother lode of some
History.

The War on Poverty or on the people of Viet Nam.
Take capsules of history.
Hear LBJ make a point
With jokes on Texas lions
Or Lady Bird feed dreams of palaces and flowers
In a nasal, drawling voice.
Read repository newspapers:
The Great Society legislated
Out hunger, discrimination, injustice.
Experience traveling into space
And be proud.

I heard the helicopter landing
On the roof
And the Chief Executive who was
Enter the pretend Oval Office
— One eighth in size even smaller
In function —
To reminisce on what went wrong.

The glaring red boxes still challenge
But, there is stark silence
In the perfectly conditioned and lit
Womb.

Patricia Roberts Yaeger

THE FRAILTY OF MAN

The diagnosis was Waldenstrom — good blood going bad —
disease rare, cause unknown, prognosis fatal.

And so the battle raged: sick cells rubbing on
weak ones deep in the catacombs of Adam's flesh,
my Adam, my world. My whole world was suffering
in '72, for Adam and Texas had cancer and I came to
grips with the frailty of man. All was not well
in Eden. The snake in the garden was Sharp and the

apple he dangled was gold and one apple tempted two
dozen trusted men. Macromoney was as malignant as
Macroglobulinemia Waldenstrom. Sharp offered quick
profits to powerful friends in return for new banking
laws and they bit. From the governor on down they bit.
And their nakedness shamed us all. The Sharpstown

Stock Fraud Scandal exposed a pork barrel full of
worms. By Fall the transgressors were politically
dead; the body count mounted as November neared. One
by one they fell from grace and turned to dust. As
shock waves droned on, the tenacious Dirty Thirty ground
the scandal's bitter fruit into reform; and a laissez-

faire electorate got off its sprawling butt and
cleaned House with an angry broom. We lost faith
and charity and almost hope, but East of Eden we chose
Old Law And Order Nixon to lead us out of chaos while
Democrats called the whole thing a Republican Plot.
So much for hope. That was the year of Dirty Tricks.

The diagnosis was greed — good blood going bad —
disease rare, cause unknown, prognosis fatal.

Joyce Pounds Hardy

FOUNDATION OF ROCK

Sleep quietly, you once strong adventurous souls,
The quiet, small county carved from other larger ones
Has found it still can draw those who seek a change
From masses in crowded city streets
To find a home of boundless reams
Where they can plan and grow a dream.

Rest easily, you forward looking pioneers —
We who came later never were to know —
Yet names slip easily off our lips,
Boydston, Elgin, Royse, Heath, Jones, Barnes, Manson, Bowles,
You traveled rutted, slippery roads
To claim a title for this tiniest Texas block
Named for stones beneath the soil where still we walk.

Sleep on and be happy, you gentle ones,
Changes have come — no more the mules plow through the tough black earth,
No more the prairie grasses grow too high to hide a man.
Sound of motors fill the hills and flat land
Where few farms and ranches still are seen.
We now sail the lake where once were fields and trees,
Concrete, houses, water are the rule.
Yes, one hundred years have brought a change,
We call it progress — no more can we say "home on the range."

Lie in peace, you pioneer men and women
Who tamed this black prairie land,
And left your names in memory and progeny.
Today, 1973, people in this place
You journeyed tortuous miles to claim
Complete 100 years as a county — Rockwall is the name.

Gene Scogin Crawford

1974

SLICK DELIVERY

Like addicts,
hooked on speed,
we line up behind gas pumps,
fuming over the hassle
in pumping a quick fix.

What's the deal?
If one source is dry,
we'll rig a fresh one out of the ocean,
put the heat on rocks
if necessary.

Who can think of cutting supply
while there's demand for one last smuggle,
a slick delivery,
rushing through our pipelines,
its vapors gathering to power our heady drive.

Rebecca Gonzales

1975

LUBBOCK, TEXAS: JANUARY 22, 1975

In five hours the sun will blow in cold,
the first snow whirl down from Amarillo
carloads of in-laws claiming first to reach the *little mother,*
phone back home: "It's twins! Hot damn, you outta see 'em!"
and scatter camp between the icebox
and Great Aunt Sarah's tribal divan
at home with whichever one's too newly married
to turn it down.

But now she's swollen in the platform rocker
her husband's mother dusted from the attic
when she heard the pregnant news.
A perfect fit for babies and grandmothers.
It's early yet; the dark
cold inside this quilt of wedding rings —
another gift of consequences
vague about the heavy thighs, the inland sea
that's burst its banks between the bed and toilet.

Too soon. The doctor promised April
but organs press against her heart
crowding out their plans,
her sleeping husband's schedule. How can she wake him
now to say it's time? He'll dare ask if she's sure,
ignore the sticky floor, her center of gravity
dropped too low to bend the knees.

He is so sleepy.
The G.I. Bill makes no allowance for babies.
Danang is falling in the recent papers.
Sometimes at night he laughs out names
light as waterlilies, translucent bubbles of exotic fish.
By day he sulks between his classes and their rented house,
comes home angry at nobody
he snaps, pacing out a speech in the kitchen
while she tries to eat the casserole
her mother warned she'd need.
THE WAR. THE GOVERNMENT. THE JOB MARKET.
CORPORAL SMITZER WHO WILL VANISH RIGHT BEFORE YOUR EYES.
She begs him softly to a chair. His tuna's getting cold.

But now he's curled tight as a bean
in no hurry to open, unlike the blossom
in her belly, its time-release speeded up
for all to see, even her husband
stretching out of bed, puzzled at the suitcase
by the crib he means to put together in a month.
A tinny static rouses him to Run! Run!
Form your troops! The perimeter's breached!
The walls are tumbling down!
No S.O.P. for the middle of the night.
No time to be afraid of all the years
he'll have to recollect this death-defying act.

Robert A. Fink

HISTORIC PARALLELS

Under Texas skies in bicentennial summer
they raised the battle flag of Bennington,
proud heritage of the revolution that turned
thirteen colonies into thirteen states, united.

Two flags flew in Austin, the capitol city,
the victory flag of Bennington; Texas Lone Star,
icon from her own revolution, when she
lost battles; won a war; won a peace;
a republic as unique as the robust Texans
who roped and dogged and branded her
three bars and a star; then turned her out
to pasture on two hundred sixty seven thousand
square miles of cedar, sand, and sage,
seacoast, mountains, and prairies, before
she drew a bill of giving, loosening her Lone Star
into cosmos of country;
her colors, bars and stripes merging before
the stars and stripes of union.

Three flags streamed in Texas skies;
historic parallels blending into one vast
diorama of colonies, republic, states that
together formed reservoirs of strength unparalled in history.
One entity; one flag symbolic of each, symbolic of all;
embracing, inspiring, protecting
one people, indivisible.

Auta Lee Reed

1977

WHEN MORNING COMES

[*September 1977 — We have just arrived in Austin to live here. I have met a few writers already. Reading one of them, it surprises me to know that there are two horned toads. I will write a poem on the prince-toad.*]

These banks
where I live
will become other that grow
close up to the trunk,
to the branches
and the candid serrated leaves
in the right green of a joyful hour.

When mornings come,
joyful, joyfully
in the bright red
of wild strawberries —
not only the toads
will feed
or so they say.

Near the banks
the velvet of his flesh
beneath bluegreen skin
in the warm, fresh,
still hours,
a syncopated prince
enjoying
the elements of day.

If only these wild strawberries
could let us see ourselves
men and women —
eternal toads —
lovers or beloved
forever scorned.

Cecilia Bustamente

Translated by Professor Maureen Ahern and the author.

BARBARA'S RETURN

Female, black and broke
seemed like a triple whammy
of some fickle fate

Professor Jordan
through typical Texas grit
proved this is untrue

When Congresswoman
she won a million hearts in
one keynote address

When in the classroom
the higher ethics mesh with
down-to-earth logic

Finding the right words
might activate the goodness
latent in the world

She has dignity
of great silences and speaks
for integrity

In sorrow or joy
her voice with a symphony
stirs the bone marrow

She can smell motives
so rascals in sheep's clothing
seek more naive game

Knowingly she smiles
when reality intrudes
on complacency

Mentally we see
and note skin tones differ
— incidentally

Claudia Nabors

1979

GOING ON

[*We'll come back from this. We'll go on. — Wichita Falls resident, after April 10, 1979 tornado.*]

Forever witnessing
that moment when the storewindows
billowed like sails and burst
in a whirl of glass,
the mannequins at Sikes Center mall
recoil, as if in a tableau of terror,
their wigless heads askew,
their torsos and arms
wrenched into macrabre poses.

But the living, trying to forget,
go on. For years they will wake
suddenly in the night, the bedclothes
twisted around them. For years
thunderheads will find them
trembling in bathtubs or closets,
their eyes squeezed shut.

But now, sorting through rubble
in the morning light,
they marvel at the random
or miraculous — the cinderblock
skewered by a broomstraw,
the china closet spared
in a roofless house —
and salvage what they can.

Holding each other, glad to be alive,
they watch the sky, and turn
to what the future holds,
forever changed,
like the cracked cups they will drink from,
gently, with both hands.

Daryl Jones

1980

QUARANTINE — CHRISTMAS

Already decorations fly into place, lurid horses
(neighing colored lights) paw, windows abound,
tinselly carols — all to cushion the Yule shock,
infuse the city with its neon venom,
protect its healthy popcorn and intolerance
against the furious monkeyshines and the fanatics
bled white as a prime star in a wistful sky.

Numbing the spirit eases the party through
thickets of celebration of a miracle
Wise Men came from far countries with lollipops to kiss.
Globes and the tutti-frutti dazzle of a million volts
usher a city through the crystal arabesque
corded and veined with eye-popping lights,
some strung on cranes lit atop buildings downtown,
some toyed on, off, quartz-true, at a remote spot.

The pestilence of Christmastide toggles this quarantine
to neutralize the heart and to hustle
worshippers adrift through Christmas crisis
on pain of yielding under supreme stress
to hullabaloo gaudy in the eastern mode
that once turned the world around and left it God-sick.

Archibald Henderson

1981

MARSHA AND THE POETS

[*If I had a wife, and if I were painting or making poems, I should simply forget her existence for days at a time. And you know well that no loving woman would put up with such a husband very long.*

— Kahlil Gibran]

Finally, we get to Paul's. Two days
on the road. We've seen the landscape change
So when we drive up, when we finally see Paul,
the sun is sinking lower than the cottonwoods
around his house.
We all sit around the big
oak table in his dining room and we begin
with Lone Star and it goes down smoothly,
soothes our throats, loosens our tongues.
It stimulates the poetry in us, makes it rise.
Marsha moves mostly in the shadows
in and near the dark corners of the rooms.
She dusts the piano,
washes the dishes,
folds the clothes,
keeps three-year-old Phyllis occupied,
out of the way from the poets.
Once, I hear the child cry
in a bedroom upstairs.
We drift away from poetry,
We tell nasty jokes about traveling salesmen,
Aggies, women who like to tease men,
and we laugh a crude macho laugh.
Once, when Marsha glides by us, silent as the moon,
Morris catches her by the arm,
invites her to come sit with us,
to drink and to talk with us.
She tells him she'll join us shortly,
that she's going to check on Phyllis upstairs,
that maybe she will have a beer before she goes to bed.
There are bluebonnets on the beer mug
that Paul drinks from —
a beautiful Texas Hill Country scene,
a flowing stream,
crystal clear water,
deep blue sky,
cedar covered hills.
I notice all this detail
when Marsha returns for her beer.

David Yates

[Excerpted from his longer poem, "Marsha and the Poets" Limited Edition.]

OUR LADY OF GUADALUPE

December 12
at 3 o'clock
in the morning
the people
of Guadalupe Parish
celebrate
her birthday,
a thousand rose petals,
velvet cool scent
against night air,
an aztec drum
vibrates
The goddess does not fade.
Roses, Roses,
on the altar, in the aisle,
in people's arms,
singing.
Roses
in the cold dead
of winter.
Guadalupe came before Juan
Diego time after time. Said
tell the Bishop to build me a
shrine here.
On the first Saturday
in September,
a pig farmer, some men
who work in a cement
factory, some men
from the parish,
and
a young girl (whose
great grandparents
gave land to the
parish so
Guadalupe church
could be built,
whose name the
sparkling nuns from Ireland
do not know,
who has lived all
her life in the
ancient house
out back of
the church,
who is Guadalupe)
gather.

They rehearse a
play 500 years old,
a medieval pageant
play that came
from Spain to Mexico
to San Antonio.
Her image falls into the tangle
of our lives. Bring candles to
celebrate her birthday,
candles and roses.
They rehearse
in the backyard
of the church
to perform in November
and December
all over town
in schools and
in back yards,
in rain and snow,
weekends and
at night
always out doors
No matter what kind of
weather they play
out the pageant.
Their voices are
mumbled. The play
is in Spanish.
It was printed
for the first time
in the 1970s.
The loudest voice
is Lucifer.
The director
plays Lucifer.
He once led
a sacred dance
troupe.
His magic is
astonishing.
Los Pastores in
New Mexico is
directed by
his cousin.
The design on
his cape
is the head
of a free dragon.
He has given
that cape
to his son
and is making
a new one.
Juan Diego said the bishop
would pay no attention to
him, said he was no one.
Roses and candles,
candlelight and
the barrio,
a cold winter
morning,
3 a.m.
in Mexico City
at the shrine of
Guadalupe, the image
of Juan Diego is
cast across the
iris of the eye
of the goddess.
Some say the cloth where her
image still holds is a contract
between indigenous and
European peoples.
Singing.
The shrine
of the Aztec Saint,
alive as a rose,
pulls
nutrients
from civilizations
entwined
like plants
and the earth.

Susan Bright

FLIGHT OF THE EARTH WOMAN
LIFT OFF

Whirling into the onyx shade
petticoat clouds miles away
between blue/green world
and moon hollow glade:
Sally Ride, Sally Ride.

Woman (the Soul)
of Space Shuttle ride
claiming her place in technological skies.
Through kitchen windows other minds fly:
Sally Ride, Sally Ride.

Like the locus traveling orbit of Self
flight of free thought off gravity's shelf
and America's pride wears
the red, white and blue:
Sally Ride, Sally Ride.

From the Lone Star State
June 18th, 1983
"Houston, we've got lift off" becomes reality.
Leaving her mark on the wings of our heart:
Sally Ride, Sally Ride.

Susan W. Daubenspeck

THE WAR OF '84

The arrows tipped with words of gore
So sharply barbed and painted for
The battle of the animals,
The Texas struggle in the war.

The Donkey and the Elephant
Were as it was with Lee and Grant
Except the combat, bloodlessly
While still replete with strife extant.

The year was 1984,
A year of promises galore
When each was right and each was best,
To listen to each orator.

Voting done and ballots counted,
Speech and travel now surmounted,
All was ended, all was over,
Few had need to be recounted.

The Pachyderm in seemed stampede,
Had crushed the Donkey without heed
For resident incumbency,
And mirrored well the nation's deed.

The promises are left to dwell
In minds of those who listened well
To see if what was said would be
Or if each pledge succumbs with knell.

The elected only and time will tell!

Marvin Hirsh

1985

ON A WEEKEND IN SEPTEMBER

Come God
be man woman child old one
bread breast of the world and water
for that matter
lamb stretched down and down down to the meanest grub
struggling to swim on concrete

merged into mortal stuff
Ancient of Days of Seas
mirroring
hauled to your hard wood
Creator brought to creature

here where I remember Lee Palmer
who 80-odd years ago
prayed by no book but that terrible book of the deeps
on a weekend in September
I quickly skimmed

> *Dear Jesus*
> *make the waters recede*
> *and give us a pleasant day tomorrow to play*
> *and save my little dog Youno*

nobody remembers Lee Palmer now
why would they
he would be an old man now
dying maybe senile maybe
nobody would like him and would wish to hell he'd hurry

still I hope
Lee Palmer
swept out from Galveston in 1900
was swept up to you on the Gulf's gray tongue

because were one lapped
and lulled in the very body of the beloved
that were not bedding deep enough for one to know
and be known back

when each should tremble
cradled in the other's memory
shifting
such risky ocean

Open Sea
whose sides
eye cannot touch

Vassar Miller

Reprinted permission *Poetry Magazine*

MESSAGE TO OUTER SPACE

"*Yipee! Ride 'Em Cowboy!*"
"What's it with you, Tex?"
"Just heard from Houston Mission Control —
we're celebrating the Sesquicentennial."
"What's that?"
"Aw, come on, Gorki! You Russians know
Texas won its independence from Mexico,
one hundred and fifty years ago!"
"Sure."
"This whole year we'll be celebrating
with jamborees, festivals, roundups,
contests like horseshoe and cow
chip throwing, square dancing.
What I wouldn't give to get my gal
by my side and do the *Cotton Eyed Joe*.
Look you kick and . . . Ouch!"
"Don't you know your space station's
limitations by now?"
"Yeahhhh . . . and a rodeo! Just to feel
that buckin' bronco once again. You
haven't ridden any spaceship that bucks
and rolls like them critters."
"Sounds tiring."
"No, man, it's exhilarating
as you Russians would say.
And you haven't eaten anything like that
Texas barbecue. I can close my eyes and
smell it now with red beans, slaw . . .
jalapeño corn bread . . . And Willie Nelson
commanding a Jamboree. Oh what I wouldn't
give to be at those root'n toot'n celebrations.
It's like the *big bang* up here. Yeahhhh . . .
it's a great time to be a Texan."

Peggy Zuleika Lynch

PRESENTING THE POETS

Adams, Faye Carr, Dallas. The Corresponding Secretary of the Poetry Society of Texas, and a former Poet Laureate of Texas. Among her published works, *More Than A Loaf* is her favorite.

Anderson, Patty O'Briant, League City. A computer programmer at the LBJ Space Center. As an avocation she writes and publishes her poetry.

Appelbee, Evelyn Corry, Henderson. Proprietor of the "Country Trader Wood Stove Store." Her favorite among her published works is *Let Rocks Their Silence Break,* which won the Nortex Book Publication Award, PST, 1981.

Baass, Mildred Vorpahl, Victoria. A partner in "Baass Originals," ceramicist and designer. *Mythology In Verse* is her favorite published book. She is a Fellow in the International Academy of Poets.

Bair, Nova Schubert, Amarillo. Her major interest lies in church work and creative writing classes. She has published *Where Jesus Walked,* her favorite. She finds time to help other poets as Councilor, PST.

Barney, William D., Fort Worth. Now retired from the Post Office Department. *The Kildeer Crying* is the favorite among his published works. He was the recipient of the Robert Frost Memorial Award, Poetry Society of America, 1962 and a Past Poet Laureate of Texas.

Barton, Jim Tom, Austin. Retired from business, his interest lies in writing prose and poetry in the field of Texana. *Eighter From Decatur* is his prose work while his poetry may be found in collections and poetry magazines.

Beamer, Mary Walker, Denton. Her major activity is teaching a large Bible class. She was selected Poet Laureate, Texas Federation of Women's Clubs in 1955 and again in 1970.

Behlen, Charles, San Antonio. He teaches creative writing as a vocation with poetry as his avocation. *Perdition's Keepsake* is his favorite published work. He was nominated for the Pushcart Prize for Poetry, 1980.

Benton, Gilbert, Alvin. Professor of English, Alvin Community College. His fields are composition, literature and creative writing.

Birkelbach, Alan L., Plano. A sales representative. Poetry is his avocation and he enjoys the competition in the Poetry Society of Texas. His poetry has been published in collections and poetry magazines. He is now working on his poetry book.

Bowman, Roberta Pipes, Fort Worth. She is active in writing both poetry and prose. Her book *In This Our Times* is her favorite. She has received international and local awards for her poetry.

Brady, Beth Bryant, Austin. As a writer of both prose and poetry she has earned a number of awards by the Poetry Society of Texas.

Bright, Susan, Austin. An Art-based Learning Consultant, poet, writer and publisher. She has worked with the program artists in the schools and is the Founding Director of Texas Circuit. In the course of her work she has given numerous poetry readings.

Brisbin, John B., Spring. A publisher of intellectual, general interest and investment newsletters with poetry as an avocation.

Burlingame, Robert, PhD, El Paso. His interest lies in teaching and writing. *Eighteen Poems* is his favorite poetry book and he has been nominated for the Pushcart Prize.

Bussey, Ruby Hughes, Pasadena. She is family oriented, active in PST and its local chapters. An active competitor for various PST awards, she took First Place in The President's Award, 1984.

Bustamente, Cecilia, Austin and Peru. Her forte is writing against the clock. Among her published works *The Names of Things* is her favorite. She was awarded the National Prize for Poetry — Peru, 1965, the first woman to receive that prize.

Butts, J. G., Midland, an accountant. In addition to writing poetry she is a rose show judge. Also, she is a student in Midland College and won the Midland College Creative Writing Contest, 1984.

Calkins, Jean, Farmer's Branch. Editor of *Jean's Journal* devoted to poetry. Among her published works, *Beyond Verse,* a text, is her favorite.

Canizaro, Mary, Kempner. Her major interests lie in teaching and mothering with poetry as an avocation. She has received several first place awards in the contests sponsored by PST.

Carmichael, Irene, Rockwall. A free-lance writer with interest in historic themes for writing prose and children's poetry. Her poetry has appeared in several collections and newspapers.

Carrico, Gladyse Bryan, San Antonio. She is active in the San Antonio Council of Presidents and was selected as Poet Laureate, Alamo District, Texas Federation of Women's Clubs, 1982. She also paints in various media.

Caulkins, Esther Mtr., Austin. She is active in Poetry in the Arts, a series of monthly poetry readings held in Austin, and in the work of PST. *Cornucopia* is her favorite among her published works.

Child, Cecil L., Austin. A retired building designer. Poetry has become his greatest pleasure in retirement. Among his published works, *Observations* is his favorite. He competes successfully in state and local poetry contests.

Cole, Terry J., Austin. Who operates his own business, Art and Graphics, with poetry as a hobby. The favorite among his published works is *Reaching: The Greatest Chance to Bend.*

Colquitt, Betsy, PhD, Fort Worth. Professor of English, Texas Christian University and Editor of *Descant. Honor Card and Other Poems* is her favorite among her published works. In 1980, she received the AddRan College of Arts and Sciences, Publication Award, TCU.

Combs, Dorothy E., Austin. A longtime writer of prose and poetry. She is competitive and an award winner in contests sponsored by the Austin Poetry Society and PST.

Cortez, Teresa McDonald, Pharr. Her vocation is that of a reporter with the *Pharr Press* and her hobby is poetry. She is proud of "Man-made Monsters," a sestina.

Craven, Jerry, PhD, Canyon. Professor of English, West Texas State University and Editor of *Separate Doors,* a journal of contemporary poetry. Among his published works *The Last Running* is his favorite.

Crawford, Gene Scogin, Rockwall. Presently editing the Rockwall County History with the Rockwall County Historical Foundation. Poetry is her hobby and her poems have appeared in several collections.

Curry, Kathleen Henry Harris, Waco. Long dedicated to God, Family and Literature. Her book *My Legacy In Song* is her favorite among her published works. She has served as Poet Laureate of Texas.

Daubenspeck, Susan W., Houston. She is now working on a book of poetry of the Sioux Indians and also writes lyrics. Her book *Flight of The Earth Woman* is awaiting publication. An active competitor, she has had numerous awards for her poetry.

Ditmore, Michael, Abilene.

Dunn, Kimo, San Antonio. A retired Army Major General who has turned his hand to writing prose and poetry, free-lance. He competes successfully in various PST poetry contests and was designated Poet Laureate, San Antonio Poet's Association, 1982.

Dunaway, Allie Merle, Austin. While her major interest for many years has been red polled shorthorn cattle, she has pursued poetry as her hobby and successfully so in numerous contests. She placed first in the National Contest, American Association of University Women.

Dykes, Weems S., Reverend, Eastland. A clergyman with strong interests in humor and poetry. *A Cup Of Thoughtfulness* is his favorite among his published works. He has been designated Poet Laureate of Texas.

Eckert, Vera L., San Angelo. A devoted great-grandmother and an active poet. Among her published works *The Legacy of Santa Fe and Other Poems of the Southwest* is her favorite. She has been designated Poet Laureate of Texas.

Elliott, Jerry C., Houston. A Project Engineer in the Space Shuttle Program working on crew equipment for astronauts. He has several poetry books ready for publication and was finalist in the Poetry Contest, Houston Festival, 1981.

Ewing, George Wilmeth, PhD, Abilene. Professor of English, Abilene Christian University. His writings include a book about verse, *The Well-Tempered Lyre: Songs and Verse of The Temperance Movement.*

Farnell, Barbara, Dallas. She is a Field Trip Specialist for the Dallas Independent School District with poetry as her avocation.

Fehler, Gene, Bergstrom AFB. Visiting Artist in Texas Poet in the Schools Program. His book *The Day Willy Missed the Bus* is his favorite. He was designated Poet of the Year in 1983 by *Spitball Magazine.*

Ferguson, Doris K., Deer Park. She combines the interests of wife and mother with those of a newspaper columnist, poet and publisher. Among her published works, *Blessings; Curses, Rhymes and Verses* is her favorite. She was the winner of the Voertman Award, PST, 1983.

Fink, Robert A., PhD, Abilene. Associate Professor of English, Hardin-Simmons University. Among his published works he considers *Azimuth Points* his favorite. In 1981 he received the Texas Review Poetry Award.

Fleming, Marie R., Nederland. Curator of the Nederland Windmill Museum, collecting and preserving local history. Poetry is her hobby.

Flowers, Betty S., PhD, Austin. Professor of English, The University of Texas.

Fowler, Zinita, Carrollton. She enjoys writing in all forms and topics. She is Co-Editor of *Crossroads,* a poetry newsletter. She has published *Ghost Stories of Old-Timers* based on her research in folklore. Also, she participates in workshops and poetry contests being a consistent winner, state and national.

Frederick, Mary Esther, Austin. She views her life as a poem and has interests in painting and sculpture. Her poems have been published in *Christmas In Texas.*

Gassman, Gladys, Austin. Seeks to express her observations and philosophy of life in poetic forms. *Poems and Pastimes* is her favorite among her published poems and her prize winning poems have been included in *Prize Poems,* National Federation of State Poetry Societies.

Gatlin, Mrs. R. E., Wichita Falls. Her interests lie in teaching Sunday school, the local poetry society and PST. Among her published works *Take Cover* is her favorite book. Her poems frequently appear in *Prize Poems,* National Federation of State Poetry Societies.

Givens, Bettye, Plainview. A teacher at the Paris American Academy, France, who also conducts workshops as a writer in the Texas Schools. The working title for her latest novel is *The Panhandle* and her favorite among her published works is *Red Headed Tree.*

Gonzales, Rebecca, Groves. She has had poetry published in *Cedar Rock* and her poetry book in process is to be published by Prickly Pear Press.

Griffin, Larry D., PhD, Midland. A professor at Midland College teaching creative writing. He has published two books of poetry, *New Fires,* his favorite.

Grundy, Ruth, Dallas. A retired journalist and teacher of piano and voice who now applies her talents to the techniques of writing poetry. *The Poetic Cake Baker* is descriptive of that effort. She is a consistent winner in poetry contests both state and national.

Haas, Nina M., Houston. Her business is "Antique Gazebo" and poetry is her hobby. *Landscapes* is her favorite among her published works.

Hagstrom, Joy Gresham, Burkburnett. The center of her interest is teaching children Christian principles through poetry and she has produced *Teaching Stories In Rhyme,* books one through three being published. She has been designated Poet Laureate of Texas.

Hammes, Ken, PhD, Cisco. Professor of English and Chairman of the Department of Language and Communication, Cisco Junior College.

Handley, Shirley Jones, Johnson City. Chairman of the Committee for Poetry in the Schools, PST. She teaches poetry in the enriched school programs both public and private. Her poetry has appeared in many collections and anthologies.

Hansen, Dorothy Lee, Mineral Wells. A fourth generation Texan who has been teaching English in California. Now back home, she does poetry readings, being scheduled for Austin and Houston. Her latest poetry book about Texas is *Cedar Berries.*

Hardy, Joyce Pounds, Houston. She is active in Campus Affairs, Rice University and Past President, Association of Rice Alumni. She received the Texas Writers Recognition Award, The Texas Institute of Letters, 1981.

Henderson, Archibald, PhD, Houston. Professor Emeritus of English, University of Houston. *Where You Are Now* is his favorite among his published works.

Henderson, Thomas J., Hale Center. A retired farmer who switched to poetry after he retired. *A Walk In The Woods* is his favorite among his published works.

Hensey, Fritz, PhD, Austin. An Associate Professor, The University of Texas, his field is linguistics, teaching, research and writing. His work is primarily published in collections.

Hill, Bessie May, Austin. Retired from the Texas Interscholastic League Foundation, The University of Texas, she pursues her interest in writing, especially poetry. Her poetry is widely published in various journals and collections.

Hirsh, Marvin, DDS, Garland. A general practitioner of dentistry and Vice-President of the Poetry Society of Texas. He is interested in a variety of poetic forms and gives demonstrations and readings. His book *In The Eyes of The Children* is now in preparation.

Hoggard, James, PhD, Wichita Falls. Professor of English, Midwestern University. Among his published works, *Two Gulls, One Hawk* and *The Shaper Poems* are his favorites. He has received the Hart Crane and Alice Crane Williams Memorial Fund Award.

Houston, Opie R., Austin. He is presently teaching poetry in the Austin Community College, Lifetime Learning. *Muses and Contemplations* is his favorite published work. He is a competitive poet and has been awarded numerous first places at the state and national level.

Huffstutler, Mickey, Edna. A retired school teacher who finds poetry her present way of life and outlet for her creative efforts. *Lord Keep Me Warm* is her favorite of her published works. She has been designated Poet Laureate of the Texas Federation of Women's Clubs.

Jones, Daryl, PhD, Lubbock. Professor and Chairman of the Department of English, Texas Tech University.

Jones, Joseph, PhD, Austin. Professor Emeritus of English, The University of Texas. He considers language our sovereign gift and seeks to use it well in all forms of expression, especially poetry. Among his published works *Ecology XVII* is his favorite. He takes pleasure in having originated the term "seventeener."

Kallsen, T. J., PhD, Nacogdoches. Distinguished Professor of English (Emeritus) Stephen F. Austin State University. *Making: Selected Poems* is his favorite. He is distinguished for the first group of concrete poems published by *College English.*

Kirkland, Margie, Lufkin. A free-lance writer who considers *Love Runs Deep* her favorite among her published works. She is Poet Laureate for Lufkin and Angelina County, named by the City and County Commissioners.

Klipple, Georgia Earnest, Austin. Her interest lies in the rearing of two grandchildren and the writing of poetry and prose, with poetry a lifelong hobby. Her prize winning manuscript, *Commencement Address,* was published in Charleston, Illinois. She is a competitive poet and has won numerous awards at the state and national level.

Land, Beatrice M., Garland. The highlight of her work in poetry has been her service as Coordinator for the Annual Student Festival in June held by the Poetry Society of Texas in Dallas. *Forget Me Knots* is her favorite among her published works and she takes pride in besting others to have her poem selected for *Poetry-Dallas.*

Leonard, Colleen Church, Midland. A teacher of piano, theory and organ who derives great pleasure in poetry. She was elated to place first in the 1982 Poetry Award, the Texas Association of Creative Writing Teachers with "The Buttermold."

Long, Virginia, Houston. She writes in various modes but mainly in poetry. *The Armadillo From Amarillo* is her favorite book of poems. She has had four poems included in the *Anthology of Magazine Verse,* 1980–1985.

Lubbe, Catherine Case, Dallas. Director Emeritus, the Poetry Society of Texas and a poet of many distinctions, among them Past President of the National Federation of State Poetry Societies. Also, she has addressed the World Congress of Poets, 1981. She is now collecting her poems for publication in book form. They had appeared in various anthologies, collections and poetry magazines.

Lynch, Peggy Zuleika, Austin. Engaged in all facets of poetry, writing, judging, editing, lecturing and publishing. The favorite of her published work is *Stacks and Files.* She is Co-editor of *A Book of The Year,* the Poetry Society of Texas and Co-editor of the anthology *Behold Texas* which was selected for inclusion in the Time Capsule celebrating the Centennial of The University of Texas, 1983.

Mahan, Budd Powell, Dallas. A Director of the Poetry Society of Texas and Chairman of the Extension Committee. He finds his major interest in volunteer work for human rights. He is a competitive poet and has been awarded numerous first places at state and national level.

Malone, Guy, Dallas. An Honorary Vice-president of the Poetry Society of Texas now retired from business and working in his garden and playing the organ. *All Fours* is his favorite poetry book and "Let Peace Rain" his favorite poem.

Marvin, Conrad W., Houston. Now retired and a student at the Glassell School of Art to develop his skill in sketching and painting in oils. Poetry is his hobby.

Marvin, Jean H., Houston. Her interests include being a poet, children's writer and homemaker.

McCormick, John Halliday, San Antonio. Now fully retired from business and as a Major General, United States Air Force. Poetry has been his hobby over the years and his favorite published poetry book is *My Feet Are Strangers.*

McDonald, Walter, PhD, Lubbock. Director of Creative Writing, Texas Tech University. *Anything, Anything* is his favorite poetry book of those published. His book *Caliban In Blue,* won the Voertman Award for the best book of poems by a Texan, 1977.

McGaughy, Mary Stallard, Fort Worth. Promotes poetry as a performing art and is helpful to other poets. She is now working on another poetry book. *The Day After* has been published and is her favorite. She is a Founder-Fellow of IAP, London, England, 1977.

McLeod, Milt, Houston. A mechanical contractor and engineer with poetry as an avocation. His poems have been published in *The Archer, Lapis, Salome* and *Touchstone.*

McNeil, Marianne McFarland, Amarillo. Her interest has been in organizing and working with a writing group for senior citizens. Her efforts have been rewarded as several members of the group have had poems published in national publications. *Mother Nature and Father Time Conspire* is her favorite published work. She won a first place in the Mississippi Poet Laureate Category 1983.

Miller, Vassar, Houston. Her present activity is editing an anthology *Despite This Flesh; The Disabled in Stories and Poems,* scheduled for publication summer 1985. Her favorite published book is *Struggling To Swim On Concrete.* She is Poet Laureate of Texas and was nominated for the Pulitzer Prize in 1984.

Mitchell, Robby K., McKinney. A Councilor for the Poetry Society of Texas working to support the society and manager of real estate as a vocation. Her book *Mockingbird's Song In The Night* is her favorite. She has been designated Poet Laureate of Texas.

Monaco, Patricia Reinhardt, Dallas. A teacher in Garland who enjoys writing poetry and who earned a first place in the 1984 Annual Awards sponsored by PST.

Moorhead, Ann Matthews, Wichita Falls. Her activities cover a wide range as a homemaker and poet. Her poetry has appeared in a number of anthologies and poetry magazines. Her poem "The Ragtime Man in The Gold Bar Room" appeared on the back cover of Danny Griffith's 14th Album.

Morris, Evelyn McDaniel, Austin. Her primary interest is the genealogy and social history of the Old South and she is a member of the University Chapter of the National Honor Society for History, Phi Alpha Theta.

Murchison, William M., Austin. His interests lie in poetry and oil painting. *Meditations For Life* is his favorite among his published books.

Murphy, Jack E., Dallas. Past President of the Poetry Society of Texas and now President, National Federation of State Poetry Societies. His major interest is to write and to promote poetry. Of his several published poetry books, *The West Side of The Mountain* is his favorite. This book won the Nortex Press Book Publication Award, PST, 1983.

Murphey, Joseph Colin, EdD, Gainesville. He is a full-time writer producing poetry, plays and novels, and was Poetry Editor for *Southwest Review,* 1964–1966. *A Return to The Landscape* is his favorite among his works.

Nabors, Claudia, Austin. Seeks to capture humility as she writes poetry, with preference to haiku. Her poetry book *Olio: Poems, Haiku and Senryu* is her favorite. Among her rewards is a first place in *Encore,* and satisfaction of seeing her poetry in numerous publications.

Nelms, Sheryl L., Hurst. An insurance examiner whose hobby is writing. *Their Combs Turn Red in The Spring* is her favorite among her published works. She placed first in the Schultz-Wyerth Award, South Dakota State University, 1978.

Newton, Violette, Beaumont. A working poet who writes, judges and publishes. Her major interest is to promote poetry as a performing art and she enjoys giving poetry recitals. *A Cathedral Ringing: Poems of Guatemala* is her favorite published book. She has been designated Poet Laureate of Texas and won the Nortex Press Book Award. PST 1980, with *The Scandal.*

Novak, Lynn, PhD, Wichita Falls. Teaches comparative literature at Midwestern State University. She is both a scholar and translator. Her poems have been published in *Descant, Pawn Review, Travois,* the *Bicentennial Collection of Texas Poetry,* and *Texas Poetry.*

Ogle, N. W., Anna. He describes his major interests as home building to feed the body; poetry to feed the soul; and, service to the First Baptist Church as deacon. His poetry has won numerous awards in both state and national poetry contests.

Oliphant, Dave PhD, Austin. Senior Editor of Publications, the Harry Ransom Humanities Research Center, The University of Texas. *Footprints, 1961–1978* is his favorite poetry book. He actively supports poets by publishing their poetry through his *Prickle Pear Press.*

Ownby, Jenna V., Amarillo. Publishes her own poetry and conducts Books by Mail for the handicapped and shut-ins, plus lecturing on poetry in the high schools. *Star Moods, Cloud Moods* is the favorite of her poetry books. Her poetry has received honors from the Academy of Leonardo Da Vinci in Rome, Italy and from *World of Poetry.*

Parra, Jose Luis, New Braunfels. His poems have appeared in *PAX* and *Cactus Alley.* He placed first in the Poetry Division, The University of Texas at San Antonio Writing Competition, 1984.

Payne, Vernon, San Angelo. Combines interests astronomy and poetry finding that astronomy suggests themes for his poetry. Editor and Publisher of *Cyclo * Flame* he corresponds with poets near and far.

Peregrino, Jose Flores, Austin. Editor, Center of Mexican-American Studies, The University of Texas, developing teaching materials for creative writing in the public schools. *Mesquitierra* is his favorite among his publications. He was honored by the Laredo Community College as their hometown poet in 1980.

Pouncey, Lorene, Houston. A bibliographic specialist working as a private consultant in literature: searching, verification and preparation of bibliographies. Her work has been recognized by the American Academy of Letters.

Preas, Jerry L., Midland. Teacher of automotive technology, Midland College and interested in communication. He is Chairman of the Technical-Vocational Section, Texas Junior College's Annual Convention. His book of prose and poetry, *Champions and The All Americans,* is his favorite.

Quiett, Garnet, Snyder. A free-lance writer, prose and poetry, as well as a homemaker. She is President of the Scurry County Poetry Society and active in church work.

Rankin, Larry, Waco. Enjoys selling, teaching, preaching and writing. For him, preaching is a God given call.

Ratisseau, Shirley Denise, Austin (and Rockport). Writer, Editor, Historian, and Genealogist. Among her many works is the movie, *This Was the Beginning,* a 150-year history in Texas, narrated by actor Chill Wills.

Reed, Auta Lee, Austin. A retired teacher now writing poetry and active in the Austin Poetry Society and PST. *Moments Long Remembered* is her favorite among her published works, now president of the Austin Poetry Society.

Reed, Bevington, PhD, Austin. Retired educator, former Commissioner of Higher Education, State of Texas. Former president of the Austin Poetry Society. His book, *San Carlos Crossing* is his favorite.

Reposa, Carol Coffee, San Antonio. Combines the joys of motherhood with her teaching and writing. Her poetry has been preserved in the Time Capsule Exhibit, San Antonio Museum of Art, 1983.

Reynolds, Lynn Carol, Houston. General Director, Houston Contemporary Dance Company — professional dance. Active in the Houston Chapter, PST, her poem "Pendulum" placed first in their recent contest.

Ricker, Vivian, Houston. A retired attorney with interest in Texas History, particularly that of the Original Texas Navy and Captain Norman Hurd. A competitive poet, she is a consistent winner in state and national contests. *The Divided Heart* is her favorite among her published works.

Rilenge, Helen M., Fort Worth. A working poet who writes, judges, competes and helps other poets. She is a member of the Poetry Society of America, Galaxy of Verse Director, and winner of numerous awards for her poetry.

Roberts, Juanita, Amarillo. Active in Panhandle Pen Women and Writers of the Golden Spread, writers groups. Also, she paints and sings in opera workshops. Her poetry has been published in numerous collections and is now being collected for publication. She is a member of the American Association of University Women.

Robertson, Pauline Durrett, Amarillo. Teaches poetry at Amarillo College and writes on historic, poetic and social issues, including editing and publishing. Her work is exemplified by *Eve's Version: 150 Women of the Bible Speak Through Modern Poets*. She is a councilor, PST.

Rogers, Del Marie, Plano. She was a grant holder in poetry from the National Endowment for the Arts, 1974–1975. *Breaking Free* is her favorite poetry book of those published.

Ross, Ovon, Pasadena. Her vocation is that of nurse and her greatest satisfaction comes from working harmoniously with others. She participates in the annual PST contests with frequent first places as with her poem "Cords."

Sánchez, Ricardo, PhD, San Antonio. A free-lance writer and proprietor of Paperbacks . . . y Mas, a book store and gallery. Also, he enjoys poetry readings. *HECHIZOspells* is his favorite among the books he has published.

Sanders, Kirby David, Houston. A travel agent for a vocation with poetry as his passion. He has published, *Sametime, Samestation Adventures,* his favorite.

Schoonmaker, Katrin E., Austin. Writes articles, speeches, advertising and, of course, poetry. She prefers themes with Biblical, social or political import.

Schultz, Lee, PhD, Woden. Assistant Professor of English, and linguistics specialist, Stephen F. Austin State University, teaching poetry, composition and literature. An adopted member of the Tuscarora Tribe, Iroquois Nation, with tribal name *Hickory Arrow.*

Scott, Margaret Firth-Eagland, Amarillo. Her major interests in addition to poetry are the study of the *Bible,* homemaking and gardening. She was one of the five authors participating in *Eve's Version: 150 Women of the Bible Speak Through Modern Poets.*

Shively, Ruth Webber, Irving. A competitive poet and consistent winner in state and national contests. Her poetry has appeared in various anthologies and poetry magazines. Presently, she is working on a BA degree in Literature, the University of Texas at Dallas. A member of the Monthly Contest Committee, PST.

Shuford, Gene, PhD, Denton. He retired as Chairman, Department of Journalism, North Texas State University, which he established in 1945. *Selected Poems, 1933–1971* is his favorite published book.

Siegel, Marcella, Irving. Recording Secretary of the Poetry Society of Texas and Chairman of the Monthly Contest Committee with Ruth W. Shively. She writes prose and poetry and teaches creative writing to a senior citizen group.

Simon, Jacqueline, Houston. A homemaker and writer of short stories as well as poetry. Her fiction has been recognized by the Texas Writer Recognition Award.

Skaggs, James D., PhD, Austin. A professor of English, The University of Texas, teaching creative writing. Among his poetic efforts is the combination of lyrics with his musical talent. His book *Voices From The Heartland* received first prize in the National Award for Bicentennial Poetry.

Sodowsky, Roland E., PhD, Alpine. Teaches creative writing and other English courses at Sul Ross State University, and writes both prose and poetry. He received the Texas Institute of Letters Short Story Award, 1982.

Spray, Jennie, Wichita Falls. An active member of the Wichita Falls Poetry Society and a consistent competitor in state and national poetry contests who wins her share of the prizes. Her poems have been published in various anthologies, collections and poetry magazines.

Stamey, Joseph D., PhD, Abilene. Professor of Philosophy, McMurry College. His book *Ten Poems* is his favorite published work, and his poetry has "placed" in the Boston University Poetry Center Competition.

Stedman, Christine Rosamond, Austin. Her grandchildren share her interests with poetry. She is now collecting her poems with a view to publication in book form. Her poetry has received a number of first places in PST Annual Awards.

Stodghill, Pat, Dallas. Past President of the Poetry Society of Texas, Treasurer, National Federation of State Poetry Societies and a teacher of English and creative writing. Her book *Mirrored Images* won the Nortex Book Publication Award, PST, 1974. A past Poet Laureate of Texas.

Stopple, Libby, Dallas. Stimulates the creativity of children in elementary schools through sông and poetry. *A Box of Peppermints* is her favorite published book, and *Red Metal* was nominated for the Pulitzer Prize, 1954. Her poem "Abe Lincoln" appears in *Philosophy of Abe Lincoln,* a sesquicentennial book on Lincoln.

Taylor, Chuck, PhD, Austin. A professor of English, The University of Texas. He describes himself as a rock and roll poet. *Ordinary Life* is his favorite among his published works. He treasures his First Prize from the Utah Art Commission.

Taylor, Pat Ellis, Austin. A writer of prose and poetry, her book *Tonics, Teas, Roots and Remedies* is her favorite. She held a writers fellowship, National Endowment of the Arts, 1978.

Terrill, Lillian Davis, Canyon. Writes prose and poetry stressing work for children; active in the Panhandle Pen Women and Writers Association of the Golden Spread; and paints in oils and water colors. Her poem "Magic Night" took first place in the Panhandle Pen Women Contest.

Thomas, James M., Reverend, Marshall. A retired minister who has served the Poetry Society of Texas as Chairman of the Extension Committee, Director, and Councilor at Large. His poetry has been published in numerous collections, anthologies and poetry magazines.

Thompson, Esther Lee Johnson, Fort Worth. Editor of *A Galaxy of Verse,* her pride and joy. Her work provides an interchange of ideas with other poets within and outside this country. She has been honored by The Golden Laurel Leaf Crown as International Poet Laureate by the late Amado M. Yuzon.

Vaughan, John D., PhD, Marshall. President, the Poetry Society of Texas. His major interest is in promoting poetry. He is a Professor of Literature and Creative Writing, East Texas Baptist University. He placed second in the Nortex Press Book Publication Contest, 1977.

Waller, Theresa Horton, Austin. A practicing lawyer with poetry as a hobby. *A Small Gift* is the title of her poetry book.

Wells, C. J., Houston. His interests are, writing, fishing and the eternal quest for the perfect campfire and the perfect cup of coffee. He earned the T. E. Ferguson Writing Award, Stephen F. Austin State University, in 1984.

Whitbread, Thomas, PhD, Austin. A professor of English, The University of

Texas. *Whomp and Moonshine* is the favorite of his poetry books. He was awarded the Voertman Poetry Award, Texas Institute of Letters.

Willerton, Chris, PhD, Abilene. He is an Associate Professor of English, Abilene Christian University.

Williams, Patricia A. R., PhD, Houston. Associate Professor of English, Texas Southern University and Contributing Editor to *The Texas Humanist.* She edited *From The Poetic Conscience of Black Souls,* 1983.

Willis, Marjorie Burney, Houston. Retired teacher, Houston Public Schools. She now uses her M.A. degree in Fine Arts Painting and poetry. An accomplished pianist who began her studies at the tender age of three.

Wissler, Patricia, Austin. She is a busy homemaker with poetry as a hobby, active in the Austin Poetry Society and PST.

Woods, Christopher, Houston. Writes poetry, plays and fiction with no particular bias. He received a grant from Mary Roberts Rinehart Foundation and a Fellowship from the Edward Albee Foundation. His poem "Easter Sunday" was published in *The Cap Rock.*

Yates, David, New Braunfels. Well known among poets as Editor-Publisher of *Cedar Rock.* His latest book, always a favorite, is *Motions.*

Yaeger, Patricia Roberts. A Houston resident born in Arequipa, Peru. As Director of Community Relations, the Catholic Diocese of Galveston–Houston, her major interest is to bring people together to create better understanding. Poetry is her allied hobby. Her favorite book, published in Peru, is *Poemas de Antes y Despues,* 1980.

Yelton, Marjorie Ledbetter, Dallas. Director, the Poetry Society of Texas. She edited twenty-two issues of *Elm Fork Echoes* for the Peters Colony Historical Society, Carrollton. Her contributions to the work of PST were recognized in The Appreciation Award, PST, offered by Jack E. and Freeda Murphy, 1984.

POETS AND THEIR POEMS

Adams, Faye Carr — *La Reunion*	1854
Anderson, Patty O'Briant — *Christmas*	1914
Appelbee, Evelyn Corry — *A City Besieged*	1862
Baass, Mildred Vorpahl — *Texas Joins The Union*	1845
Bair, Nova Schubert — *Red River*	1864
Barney, William D. — *Judson Thrush*	1942
Barton, Jim Tom — *To Texas*	1859
Beamer, Mary Walker — *Museum Piece*	1880
Behlen, Charles — *The Ice Storm*	1949
Benton, Gilbert — *Wheeler Shannon, Texas Hero*	1853
Birkelbach, Alan L. — *The Flame, The Cross, The Sin, The Veil*	1925
Bowman, Roberta Pipes — *Dark Threatenings Grow*	1860
Brady, Beth Bryant — *The Beginnings of Higher Education in Texas*	1841
Bright, Susan — *Our Lady of Guadalupe*	1982
Brisbin, John B. — *Six-Shooter Junction*	1904
Burlingame, Robert, PhD — *Los Chisos*	1856
Bussey, Ruby Hughes — *Amarillo From Ragtown to Boom Town*	1921
Bustamente, Cecilia — *When Morning Comes*	1977
Butts, J. G. — *The Power*	1916
Calkins, Jean — *The Texas Navy*	1837
Canizaro, Mary — *September Scene*	1842
Carmichael, Irene — *Night Raid*	1900
Carrico, Gladyse Bryan — *Where are the Pioneers?*	1956
Caulkins, Esther Mtr. — *The Battle Flag at Sabine Pass*	1863
Child, Cecil L. — *A Curve in The Road*	1954
Cole, Terry — *The New Deal*	1933
Colquitt, Betsy, PhD — *Displacements — 1843 or Thereabouts*	1843
Combs, Dorothy E. — *The Last President*	1844
Cortez, Teresa McDonald — *Colors*	1970
Craven, Jerry, PhD — *Polonis Ortiz Confessing to Sergeant Wilson*	1872
Crawford, Gene Scogin — *Foundation of Rock*	1973
Curry, Kathleen Henry Harris — *Genesis of Texas*	1857
Daubenspeck, Susan W. — *Flight of The Earth Woman Lift Off*	1983
Ditmore, Michael — *The Good A Man Does*	1968
Dunn, Kimo — *Texas Contributes*	1943
Dunaway, Allie Merle — *Bastion Built*	1941
Dykes, Weems S., Reverend — *Texas: Nineteen Hundred Forty-Four*	1944
Eckert, Vera L. — *The Camels*	1855
Elliott, Jerry C. — *Grampa's Iron Horses*	1882
Ewing, George Wilmeth, PhD — *The Day of Small Things*	1851
Farnell, Barbara — *The Fifties Finale!*	1959
Fehler, Gene — *The Dispossessed*	1840
Ferguson, Doris K. — *War and Peace*	1891
Fink, Robert A., PhD — *Lubbock, Texas; January 22, 1975*	1975
Fleming, Marie R. — *In Retrospect*	1953
Flowers, Betty S., PhD — *Reconstructing Texas in* The Northern Standard	1868

Nelms, Sheryl L. — *Before and After* 1928
Newton, Violette — *Someone Must Dream The Dream* 1839
Novak, Lynn, PhD — *Eleanora In El Paso* 1884
Ogle, N. W. — *Alive In 1905* 1905
Oliphant, Dave, PhD — *John Lang Sinclair, Class Poet* 1903
Ownbey, Jenna V. — *Billy Dixon Remembers* 1890
Parra, José Luis — *The Mission* 1908
Payne, Vernon — *Timeland Waits* 1895
Peregrino, Jose Flores — *On One Quiet Bus Ride* 1967
Pouncey, Lorene — *The Year of The Women* 1918
Preas, Jerry L. — *Transitional Texas* 1969
Quiett, Garnet — *The Spirit of 1926* 1926
Rankin, Larry — *Times of Texas* 1939
Ratisseau, Shirley Denise — *The Transition, Farewell to A Way of Life* 1915
Reed, Auta Lee — *Historic Parallels* 1976
Reed, Bevington, PhD — *Incident At Battle Creek* 1922
Reposa, Carol Coffee — *Hempstead (For My Grandparents)* 1923
Reynolds, Lynn Carol — *From Brenham to Houston* 1952
Ricker, Vivian — *The Great Drought* 1887
Rilenge, Helen M. — *Lena Thayer; The Dolly Madison of The Mansion* 1901
Roberts, Juanita — *Reminiscence* 1907
Robertson, Pauline Durrett — *Quanah's Summer of Despair* 1875
Rogers, Del Marie — *The Road* 1848
Ross, Ovon — *July 19, 1889. Why This Day, Matt?* 1889
Sánchez, Ricardo, PhD — *a la 1920s* 1920
Sanders, Kirby David — *One-Eight-Six-Seven (Carpetbag Blues)* 1867
Schoonmaker, Katrin E. — *Our Camelot* 1961
Schultz, Lee, PhD — *Civilian Conservation Corps, Fort Davis* 1934
Scott, Margaret F. — *Young Cowboy To Old-Timer* 1886
Shively, Ruth Webber — *O. Henry (William S. Porter)* 1896
Shuford, Gene, PhD — *What Price?* 1947
Siegel, Marcella — *The New Cowboy* 1888
Simon, Jacqueline — *Morning, June 20, 1865* 1865
Skaggs, James D., PhD — *Round Top: Microcosm of America* 1858
Sodowsky, Roland E., PhD — *May 21, 1911* 1911
Spray, Jennie — *Fond Recollections Of A Former First Lady* 1935
Stamey, Joseph D., PhD — *Redemption To Come* 1871
Stedman, Christine Rosamond — *Padre Island (Then and Now)* 1850
Stodghill, Pat — *July 21, 1878* 1878
Stopple, Libby — *The Betsy Ross of Texas* 1929
Taylor, Chuck, PhD — *Poem to Ma Ferguson* 1927
Taylor, Pat Ellis — *Cowgirl* 1951
Terrill, Lillian Davis — *Texas, Our Texas* 1930
Thomas, James M., Reverend — *Stagecoach Road* 1846
Vaughan, John, PhD — *Death of A President* 1945
Waller, Theresa Horton — *The Cold Came Hard* 1962
Wells, C. J. — *To A Tree By A Grove* 1937
Whitbread, Thomas, PhD — *The Alcohol Question* 1912
Williams, Patricia A. R., PhD — *The Tale of Two Score and Twenty-Four* 1964

POETS AND THEIR BALLADS